Words of praise for

Biblical, personal, engaging, and thought-provoking are just a few words that come to mind when reading this wonderful book! The Virgin Mary truly is our BLESSED Mother, and listening to her words in Scripture can help us to become blessed, too. Gary Zimak has done a great service for both Catholics and non-Catholics in offering *Listen to Your Blessed Mother: Mary's Words in Scripture*, a book that unpacks the biblical words of Mary in a very conversational and easy-to-follow style. The message summary and reflection questions at the end of each chapter will be of great benefit to the reader, too! I highly recommend this book!

Donald Calloway, MIC, STL, author of *Under the Mantle: Marian Thoughts From a 21st Century Priest*

"Listen to your Mother." How many times did we hear those words growing up? How many times did we roll our eyes and ignore the sage advice only to find out later on that Mom indeed did and does know best, especially our Blessed Mother. Now, straight from Scripture, Gary Zimak has given us even more reason to pay close attention to what our Mother, as in Mary, has to say about living a grace-filled life in this world so we can be with her and her Son in the next. This book will definitely bring you closer to the heart of Christ through the Immaculate Heart of the Mother of God."

Teresa Tomeo, syndicated Catholic talk-show host and best-selling Catholic author

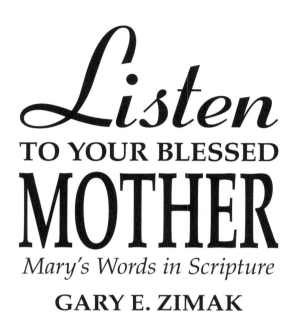

Listen
TO YOUR BLESSED
MOTHER
Mary's Words in Scripture

GARY E. ZIMAK

Foreword by Matt Swaim

Liguori
LIGUORI, MISSOURI

Imprimi Potest:
Harry Grile, CSsR, Provincial
Denver Province, The Redemptorists

Published by Liguori Publications
Liguori, Missouri 63057

To order, call 800-325-9521
www.liguori.org

Library of Congress Cataloging-in-Publication Data

Zimak, Gary.
  Listen to your Blessed Mother : Mary's words in scripture / by Gary E. Zimak.—First Edition.
    pages cm
1. Mary, Blessed Virgin, Saint—Biblical teaching. I. Title.
  BT611.Z54 2013
  232.91—dc23
                        2013018518

p ISBN: 978-0-7648-2375-6
e ISBN: 978-0-7648-6864-1

Liguori Publications, a nonprofit corporation, is an apostolate of The Redemptorists. To learn more about The Redemptorists, visit Redemptorists.com.

Printed in the United States of America
17 16 15 14 13 / 5 4 3 2 1
First Edition

Dedication

This book is dedicated to my Blessed Mother, Mary.
Thank you, Mom, for taking me by the hand
and leading me to your Son.

Ad Jesum Per Mariam!

Acknowledgments

To my beautiful wife, Eileen: Thank you for your constant love and for your support of my work. You are an absolute blessing and the best friend I've ever had. I love you!

To my wonderful daughters, Elizabeth and Mary: Thanks for being such great kids. I'm so proud of both of you, and I really appreciate how you share in my work for the Lord. Mom and I are truly blessed to have such wonderful daughters, and we love you very much!

To all of my friends in Catholic radio: There are too many of you to mention here, but know that I very much appreciate your support, as you allow me to bring the "Good News" to the airwaves.

To my friends at Liguori Publications: Thank you for allowing me to become a part of your family. Together, we have been able to reach many people, and I greatly appreciate you for letting me proclaim the Lord's message through my books.

To everyone who prayed for me as I worked on this book: All I can say is that there were many days when I felt totally dry, but the words suddenly flowed. I attribute that to your prayers, and I am very grateful for your support.

Above all, words cannot express my gratitude to Almighty God for his willingness to work through an imperfect vessel like me. May your will always be done in my life, Lord!

Foreword

Prior to becoming Catholic, I had a distorted view of Mary, mostly because I thought Catholics had a distorted view of Mary. It seemed as though Catholics treated her as a goddess (bad), or like one of those giant inflatable mascots you see in used car lots (worse). I thought they were participating in some kind of grand cultish mob misdirection, focusing on some obscure figure in salvation history, and completely blowing her out of proportion. To me, figures like St. Paul, St. James, and others deserved far more attention.

I still maintain that those men who wrote some of the key doctrinal texts of the New Testament should be read and studied by every Christian. These are people who set things down for us that are necessary to know for salvation. It's interesting, however, to note that while Mary never wrote any canonical texts herself (we don't even know if she was literate), the things she had to say were so important at crucial times in the life and ministry of Jesus that the Gospel writers (Luke, especially) saw a need to share them with us. And because of Luke's pinpoint precision gleaned through his classic medical and scientific training, none of those recorded words are accidental afterthoughts.

I mentioned that I used to think that from outside the Church, Mary seemed to loom larger than Jesus. However, from inside the Church, I've found that she shrinks down to her normal size. Her name comes up only a couple of times in the Liturgy of the Mass, and it's certainly not her I'm receiving in the Eucharist.

For me, she has stopped being some pagan demigoddess and instead has come to be what she was always meant to be: a fellow human being, preserved by the grace of God, chosen to become the model for every Christian.

When she said "yes" to God's will, she was the first to accept Christ into her heart, as even non-Catholic Christians deem to be important. However, with that "yes" she also showed her willingness to have his flesh and blood inside of her, as we who receive the Eucharist do at each Mass. When I pray the rosary in adoration, I am never tempted to visualize myself praying to Mary as though she were on the altar, but instead I envision her kneeling next to me, teaching me to see my Savior through the eyes of the one who knew him best, because she knew him before anyone else did.

As you read these reflections on Mary's words in Scripture, it is my hope that you can put yourself in Mary's sandals. Ponder what was in her heart as she spoke these words, for Luke tells us that she deeply pondered the meaning of mothering the second person of the Blessed Trinity. Her words in Scripture are few but hold powerful meaning for those willing to reflect upon them and internalize them. And if at any point you feel like she's reading over your shoulder, don't freak out: That's actually a good thing.

MATT SWAIM

PRODUCER OF *SON RISE MORNING SHOW*, EWTN GLOBAL CATHOLIC RADIO NETWORK, AUTHOR OF *THE EUCHARIST AND THE ROSARY, PRAYER IN THE DIGITAL AGE,* AND *YOUR COLLEGE FAITH: OWN IT*

Contents

Introduction

Why does Mary matter and why should we care about what she has to say? After all, if she's so important, why does she only speak on four occasions in sacred Scripture? I have a great relationship with Jesus, why do I need Mary? If you've asked these questions, you are not alone. Even among Catholics, who (for the most part) accept Mary as part of their spiritual lives, there is a lot of confusion about our Lady's role. I should know. Even though I've been Catholic all of my life, for many years I didn't understand Mary or care about what she had to say. I've since learned that I was wrong... *very* wrong. Accepting Mary as my spiritual Mother, studying her life, and listening to her words have brought me closer to Jesus than all of my previous studies and prayers. Not only is she the model Christian, but as a spiritual Mother, Mary has a profound message that she wants to share with her children. By listening to her words, we can learn to become holier and more devout Catholics. Why? Because Mary knows what she's talking about.

This book is the visible sign of a love story, one that has taken more than fifty years to develop. It is the story of how I have grown to love my Blessed Mother and how that love increases each day. Unfortunately, for most of my life it was a lopsided relationship: She loved me unconditionally, and I ignored her. Even though I knew of her, I can't say I really knew her. Over the years, I gradually began to appreciate her and learned to ask for her help. It wasn't until very recently, however, that I started treating her as a son should treat his mother: with great love and confidence. Now that I've accepted Mary as my heavenly Mother, I want to share our relationship with as many people as possible.

I was baptized into the Catholic faith as an infant and was always comfortable with the idea that Mary was an important part of being Catholic. My mother had a great devotion to her. Statues and pictures of our Lady were spread throughout the Zimak household. In fact, whenever we needed good weather for an outdoor event, it was a given that the statue of Mary was placed on the windowsill (always looking out, as if she wouldn't be able to help if she couldn't see out the window). My sister and I definitely knew about the Blessed Mother from an early age. This may sound funny, but I was very surprised when I attended my first day of classes at Maternity BVM School in Philadelphia and discovered that the Blessed Mother actually had a first name. The only name I knew for her was "Blessed Mother," and I was stunned when Sister Maria Melita referred to her by another name. Thinking I discovered a great secret, I rushed home and told my mother, "Did you know the Blessed Mother's name is Mary?" As you can imagine, my mom smiled. She did her job by planting the initial seeds in me that Mary was indeed my Mother. Although it would take many years, that seed would eventually grow and bear great fruit in my life.

All of my grandparents came from Poland, a country that had a great devotion to Mary. This probably accounts for my mother's love of the Blessed Mother. We often visited the Marian shrine of Our Lady of Czestochowa, located in Doylestown,

Pennsylvania, and I look back fondly on those trips. I especially remember the Labor Day festivals, where we ate pierogi and kielbasi and listened to plenty of polka music. More importantly, my parents always made sure we'd go inside the church and say a prayer. Surrounded by numerous images of Mary and Jesus, we prayed as a family, and peace descended upon us. With all of this exposure to Mary, it only follows that I would automatically develop a great love for her, right? In reality, nothing could be further from the truth. While I eventually grew to love Mary dearly, there was nothing automatic about that process.

Even though I had seen images of Mary all of my life and accepted her as part of being Catholic, I didn't understand her role. I barely spoke to Jesus, so why should I speak to Mary? When I did pray, I thought I'd go right to the top and speak directly to the Lord. So, what eventually led me to a healthy Marian understanding? Surprisingly it was my self-centeredness and the dissatisfaction with my life that started me on the journey. I had some real needs, and I was willing to try anything.

In 1982, I graduated from college and took a job working for the federal government. Although the salary was very low, I was happy to be employed as the economic conditions during those years were not good. For the next six years, I lived with my parents and was dissatisfied with my life. Even though my spirituality left a lot to be desired, I never stopped going to Mass, and that was a good thing. One Sunday in the fall of 1988, it was announced that our parish would be hosting a miraculous medal novena. In order to better explain what would take place at that novena, a Vincentian priest spoke at all of the Masses and gave us more information. While I would usually daydream during such talks, the priest said something that got my attention. During this novena, we would be able to ask Mary for help with our intentions, including finding a new job. Now, I was *very* interested as my two biggest intentions were finding a better-paying job and getting a girlfriend. What's there to lose, I thought—I had to give this novena thing a try.

For the next nine days, I attended the miraculous medal novena and asked Mary to help me with my intentions. My hopefulness grew stronger as the priest would read letters from people whose prayers were answered. More importantly, something he said resonated with me: "Be assured that the minute you ask Mary for something in prayer, she is immediately bringing the request to her Son, Jesus." I was completely bowled over by that statement, as I never heard anyone say that before. Suddenly, after years of praying in vain, I started to believe it was possible for my "impossible" intentions to be granted. During the novena, I sent out my first résumé and prepared to settle in for a long and painful job search, as I needed to find a higher-paying job so I could move out on my own. Although I believed the Blessed Mother could help me to find a new job, I didn't expect she would do so immediately. Within two weeks, however, I not only received an interview from that résumé but was offered a job and a fifty percent salary increase. At this point, I started to see the importance of the Blessed Mother. I viewed her as someone who could put in a good word for me with Jesus. Hardly a perfect relationship, but it was a start.

The new job enabled me to move out of my parents' house and buy a condominium. Although I still didn't have a deep relationship with Mary, I at least understood that she had a place in my life. I told my mother I'd like a statue of the Blessed Mother, and she bought me a nice one from a local religious store. I found a table and displayed Mary prominently in my condo. When I looked at her statue, I felt a sense of peace and even motherly protection. Although my new parish didn't offer a miraculous medal novena, I was very interested when they announced they were starting a young-adult group known as Twenty Something or Thereabouts. The group was devoted to praying the rosary, eucharistic adoration, and learning more about the Catholic faith, and it was geared toward younger Catholics. I'd like to say I attended these meetings because of my deep love for Jesus and Mary, but my real motivation was to meet a nice Catholic girl. What I didn't realize at the time was that the Lord was calling me to a deeper relationship with him and with his Mother. Because he knew I was spiritually immature, however, he found a way to meet me where I was at. As I attended these meetings and prayed the rosary with people my own age, I grew closer to our Lady and felt that same peace that I initially experienced at the miraculous medal novena. Although my motivation was less than perfect, I was growing spiritually.

In 1993, I met Eileen Moynahan at Twenty Something. She was beautiful, funny, and a devout Catholic. Unfortunately, she also happened to be engaged. As we got to know one another, I was extremely frustrated to find out just how much we had in common. I asked the Lord in prayer why he would make me suffer like this. After years of praying, I finally met the perfect girl for me, and she was unavailable (or so I thought). Over the weeks, Eileen and I became friends and discussed many things. I was astonished to discover she was having second thoughts about her engagement and was thinking of breaking it off. So I decided to take the bold step—and for me it *was* a *bold* step—of asking her out on a date. After an initially positive response, Eileen had some reservations and I was forced to wait. As "luck" would have it, I discovered that my former parish was having its annual miraculous medal novena. Guess where I went for the next nine days? As soon as I started to pray those familiar prayers, I felt a deep peace and accepted the fact that with our Lady's intercession, all things are possible. Although it took another month, Eileen did break off the engagement and we started dating. Then I realized more than ever that there really *is* something to the Blessed Mother's intercession.

Eventually, Eileen and I got married and, in 1997, we were thrilled to learn we were pregnant. Several weeks into the pregnancy, we were even more excited to find out (during an ultrasound) we were having twin girls. Our initial joy turned into anxiety when the doctor called an hour later to say there was a serious problem with the twins. The next day, we had a follow-up appointment and were told the girls had Twin-to-Twin Transfusion Syndrome, a very rare and often fatal condition that put their lives in jeopardy. To make matters worse, because it was discovered so early in the pregnancy, their chance for survival was very small. Without thinking twice, Eileen and I immediately started praying. Every night we would bring our statue of the Blessed Mother (the one from my condo) into the living room, light a candle, and pray the rosary. In spite of the danger, we felt incredible peace while we prayed. Twice a week we went to Our Lady of Lourdes hospital (how appropriate!) in Camden, New Jersey, for an ultrasound to see if the girls were still alive. The doctors would also measure Eileen's amniotic fluid, which would provide an indication of whether or not the problem was worsening. After an especially bad visit one day, we knew we had to name the girls. We wanted to make sure they would never be forgotten if they died. The names we chose? Mary and Elizabeth. It was our way of calling on our Blessed Mother and asking her (and her cousin) to protect our children. After riding an emotional roller coaster for several weeks, Mary and

Elizabeth Zimak were born on October 27, 1997. Despite being three months premature, the doctors could now treat their medical condition, and their chance for survival improved. We were told by several medical professionals it was a miracle they survived. Grateful beyond belief, we attributed the girls' survival to Mary's intercession. She came through once again.

Although Mary and Elizabeth are healthy teenagers today, their early years were challenging. Developmental issues and immunity concerns really knocked us for a loop. As a result, I neglected my faith. Although I continued to go to Mass, I didn't pray regularly, using the excuse that I was too tired. And, despite having been the beneficiary of the Blessed Mother's help so many times in the past, my relationship with her was still lacking. She was still just someone to turn to when I was in trouble. In no way did I view Mary as my Mother.

As the years passed, I grew to love my Catholic faith like never before. As I started to listen to Catholic radio and read more about the teachings of the Church, I heard more and more people refer to Mary as their Mother. I desired that type of motherly relationship with our Lady in my life and started to pray about it. Taking the advice of someone I heard on the radio, I asked Jesus to help me love his Mother more. In August of 2011, something happened that would put me on the right track. I was attending a Catholic Marketing Network trade show in King of Prussia, Pennsylvania, and I met Ray Mooney, who was there to promote Total Consecration to Jesus Through Mary, as popularized by St. Louis de Montfort. Ray asked me if I was interested in making the Total Consecration, and I took an information packet and said I'd think about it. I knew this devotion was very important to Blessed Pope John Paul II, and something about it was attractive to me. Deep in my heart, I wanted a better relationship with Mary, and this could be just what I needed.

On October 7, 2011, I accepted Mary as my spiritual Mother. On that day, the feast of Our Lady of the Rosary, I formally consecrated my life to Jesus through Mary. From that day on, my life has never been the same. I have grown to love Mary and turn to her constantly. She is my Mom and I am her son. Just as my own mother used to take me shopping and on various errands, Mary now takes me by the hand and leads me on the path chosen for me by her Son. And I follow with confidence, knowing that wherever Mary is…Jesus is right there, too.

Now here's the best part: Not only is Mary my Mother, but she's your Mother, too. When Jesus was dying on the cross, he looked at his Mother, standing with the Apostle John, and proclaimed to her, "Woman, behold your son" (John 19:26). Jesus then said to the beloved disciple, "Behold, your mother" (John 19:27). It has always been the Church's understanding that John represented each one of us. According to the Bible, from that hour onward, John accepted Jesus' gift and took Mary into his care. How about you? Have you accepted the gift? Are you ready to allow Mary to become your spiritual Mother?

As our Mother, Mary wants to speak to us. She longs to advise and teach us what it means to have faith and follow God's will. By listening to her words, we can learn to imitate her and grow closer to Jesus. In the pages that follow, we'll look at Mary's words and study her actions. Her greatest desire is to bring us closer to her Son. Together, let's explore our Mother's words and put them into practice in our own lives. Some have questioned Mary's importance, given that she spoke so little in the pages of the Bible. I would counter with the argument that, in those few words, she said all that needed to be said. Let's look at her words and her actions, seeing where they lead us. I have a hunch that Mary's words are going to lead you where they led me: directly to Jesus.

PART I

Spoken Words

CHAPTER 1
Seeking God's Will

"How can this be, since I have no relations with a man?"

LUKE 1:34

Have you ever been visited by an angel? Although the Church teaches that each of us has a guardian angel, most of us have never experienced what it's like to be able to see and hear an angel. In the Bible, we see several examples of angelic visits. Each of these visits has a significant purpose. In the Old Testament, Moses was given an angel to go before him and was instructed by God to "be attentive to him and obey him" (Exodus 23:21). After conceiving a child with Abram and running away, Hagar (the maid of Abram's wife, Sarai) was visited by the angel of the Lord and instructed to submit to her mistress (Genesis 16:7–9). In the Book of Judges, the angel of the Lord also appeared to the barren wife of Manoah (Judges 13:3–5) and told her she would conceive and bear a son, Samson. In the New Testament, we see numerous examples of the appearance of angels: Gabriel appearing to Zechariah (Luke 1:11–20) to announce that Elizabeth would conceive a son (John the Baptist), the angel of the Lord speaking to St. Joseph (in a dream) and urging him to take Mary as his wife, despite the fact that she was pregnant with Jesus (Matthew 1:20). The angel comforted the confused Joseph, explained that the pregnancy occurred by the Holy Spirit, and informed him that Jesus would save the people from their sins. Even our Lord himself was ministered to by angels, after he was tempted in the desert (Matthew 4:11) and while he prayed in the Garden of Gethsemane on the night before his death (Luke 22:43). By looking at these examples, we can clearly see that angels just don't show up for the heck of it. There is always an important purpose attached to their appearance.

One day, God dispatched an angel named Gabriel to a city of Galilee named Nazareth. He was sent to deliver an important message to a young virgin (Mary), who was engaged to be married to a man named Joseph. As usual, the angel arrived without warning. The Bible is silent as to where this meeting took place and what Mary was doing at the time. Was she praying? Was she performing her household chores? Was she inside the house? Was she outside?

While we have no way of knowing with certainty what she was doing when the angel appeared, we can be sure of two things. First, that the Lord reached out to Mary and sent his angel to meet her where she was. As he often does with us, God called to Mary in the midst of her ordinary duties. She didn't need to seek him out. Instead, he found her. We often forget that we can encounter God's presence while carrying out the mundane tasks of our daily lives, and this encounter reminds us it is possible. Secondly, this is the only biblical instance where an angel addresses a person by a title and not his or her proper name. While some translations say "favored one" and others "full of grace," the point remains that Mary was indeed special, and that fact was acknowledged by Gabriel in his salutation. She was chosen for a one-of-a-kind role and was about to be asked to become the Mother of the long-awaited Messiah. A role of this nature called for a special greeting that is evidenced in the angel's words.

Gabriel delivered a personal message to Mary from God. As a devout and loyal follower of the Lord, one would expect our Lady to be delighted to hear the message, "The Lord is with you." In reality, however, Scripture confirms that Mary "was greatly troubled at what was said and pondered what sort of greeting this might be" (Luke 1:29). While fear was a common reaction to the appearance of an angel, we're told that Mary was troubled at *what was said*, not by *what she saw*. We can learn much about Mary by studying her reaction to the angel's initial message. What would make her nervous about being praised and told the Lord is with her? This is the reaction of someone who is very humble. Despite the fact that she was sinless, Mary didn't feel worthy of the greeting, fully attributing all of her goodness to God's grace. This profound humility and gratitude to the Lord will be further illustrated in Mary's prayer known as the Magnificat, which we'll look at a few chapters from now.

Gabriel urged her to not be afraid and assured Mary she had found favor with God. Then he proceeded to explain the purpose of his visit, a purpose that would be enough to make most people afraid. Mary was given the details of a plan that would have her conceiving a son. That son, named Jesus, "will be called the Son of the Most High, and the Lord God will give him the throne of David his father, and he will rule over the house of Jacob forever, and of his kingdom there will be no end" (Luke 1:32–33). While you and I may look at these words and be confused as to what's being asked, a devout Jewish girl would have known exactly what was being stated. Mary was being asked to become the Mother of the Messiah!

After the angel finished speaking, Mary was confused and asked a simple question: "How can this be, since I have no relations with a man?" (Luke 1:34). Some people will look at Mary's words and wrongly conclude that her faith was weak. She'll be compared to Zechariah who, a few verses earlier, doubted Gabriel's prophecy about the pregnancy of his wife. Didn't Mary and Zechariah both doubt the angel's message? Not at all. Mary *believed* and Zechariah *doubted*. How do I know, you might ask? The answer lies in Gabriel's reaction. After Zechariah's question, the angel stated that he "did not believe my words" (Luke 1:20). Mary received no such rebuke because, unlike Zechariah, she was simply asking for details.

Sometimes we lose sight of the fact that, although Mary was sinless, she was still human. Being chosen to become the Mother of God didn't automatically give her all the answers. Like us, there were times when Mary had questions about God's will. Even though she always wanted to follow the Lord's plan for her life, she was sometimes confused and needed to discern his will. We see evidence of this when (upon Gabriel's arrival) Mary "pondered what sort of greeting this might be" (Luke 1:29). She didn't know why the heavenly messenger was visiting her. As for our Lady's question to the angel, some background is necessary in order to understand what she is asking. The common belief of many theologians through the centuries (including Blessed Pope John Paul II, St. Augustine, and St. Gregory of Nyssa) is that Mary was confused because she had consecrated her virginity to the Lord. Although unusual for married people, this practice was not unheard of in Mary's time. This theory is supported by looking at Gabriel's words. He told Mary she would conceive and bear a son named Jesus. The messenger didn't say *when*, only that it would happen at some point in time. Since Mary was engaged to Joseph, it would be expected she'd bear his children, therefore there's nothing unusual about the message...unless she vowed to remain a virgin. Always desiring to do what's right, Mary made a decision to do what she thought was best, but then Gabriel appeared with some new information. When informed that God wanted her to have a child, Mary needed to reevaluate her plan. Wanting to fulfill the will of God in her life, she needed to ask the important question. How can this be? Please tell me the details so I can cooperate with God's plan. Far from doubting, our Lady was pondering Gabriel's astonishing message and was asking for guidance in carrying out God's will.

How many times are we confused about what God wants us to do? We struggle to discern his will for our lives and we have questions. We may feel the urge to take a more fulfilling job but don't know how we'll survive on less pay. We may feel the call to the priesthood or religious life but are fearful of giving up the possibility of marriage and children. We get the idea that maybe we should volunteer and help people but don't know how. As my own life illustrates, when the Lord calls us to do something, he doesn't provide all of the details up front. For several years, I felt the call to work for the Lord as a full-time Catholic evangelist, but I didn't know how it would be possible to support my family. After an involuntary job layoff and much positive feedback, I started to follow the Lord's direction one day at a time. With Mary at my side, I continue to travel this uncertain road and ask for daily guidance. By listening to and imitating Mary's question to God's messenger, we can all learn to ask the Lord for the information needed to serve him better. As we learn to imitate our Lady, we'll be less concerned with the potential consequences and more concerned with what God wants us to do.

In addition to those instances requiring us to make a decision, sometimes we aren't given a choice. We may be faced with an unexpected illness, devastating personal problems, or financial difficulties. Although these situations occur without our consent, we often question why they are happening. How will I survive? What will I do? Why is God letting this happen?

Mary's words to the angel remind us that it's perfectly acceptable to ask questions. If you feel God is asking you to do something but you're not sure how it's possible, go ahead and ask him for details. Mary did. If you're carrying a heavy cross and can't understand why, ask the Lord to enlighten you. Unfortunately I can't promise that you'll get the answer you want. Instead the Lord's answer may be, "trust me." If that's the case, you may be asked (like Mary) to go along with his plan without knowing all of the fine details. If you have a difficult time doing that, join the club. However, always remember that Mary can help you tremendously. As someone who's been there and done that, she knows exactly what you're going through. Turn to her and ask her to share some of her faith with you. I can guarantee you that, as stated in the *Memorare* prayer to her, "never was it known that anyone who fled to thy protection, implored thy help, or sought thine intercession was left unaided."

The Message: God has a plan for my life and wants to make it known to me. Through prayer and careful listening, I can become aware of that plan and put it into action.

Reflection Questions

1. Do you feel God is asking you to do something in your life? What is holding you back?
2. How do you prepare to make a major decision in your life? Do you pray? When looking at the potential choices, do you choose based on what God wants you to do or what feels good?
3. Put yourself in Mary's place. How would you have responded to the angel's initial greeting? What would be going through your mind once you realized what he was asking?
4. Put yourself in Joseph's place. How would you react if your fiancée told you she was pregnant and you knew the child was not yours?
5. Read Luke 1:5–35. Zechariah and Mary both asked questions of Gabriel. How were these questions similar? How were they different?

CHAPTER 2

The Lord's Servant

"Behold, I am the handmaid of the Lord."

LUKE 1:38

Many times throughout my professional career as a computer programmer, I've been entrusted with confusing assignments. In an effort to ensure I did a good job, I would often ask lots of questions. How do you want this done? When do you need it by? How should we handle this or that situation if it arises? If I neglected to do this, I may head down the wrong path and end up delivering something that wouldn't meet the client's needs. Asking questions and acquiring information is generally considered to be a good thing, especially when we're performing a service for someone else.

When Mary was visited by Gabriel, she asked a valid question. Why? Because she loved the Lord and wanted to make sure she was doing what *he* wanted and not what *she* wanted. Believing that God wanted her to remain a virgin, Mary was confused by the angel's message. Always desiring to serve the Lord and do his will, Mary asked for clarification. Knowing she was sincere, Gabriel gave her the reassurance she needed while, at the same time, dropping an even bigger bombshell. First, he addressed her concern about becoming a mother while still remaining a virgin: "The holy Spirit will come upon you, and the power of the Most High will overshadow you. Therefore the child to be born will be called holy, the Son of God" (Luke 1:35).

I can guarantee I would have come back with another question at this point. Let's face it, this really doesn't make a lot of sense. It turns out Mary was right and God *did* want her to remain a virgin, but she'd also become pregnant with a child. Understandably, Mary asked the angel how this would be possible. She was told the Holy Spirit would be involved and the child would be the Son of God. A virginal motherhood? The Son of God? Are you kidding? Pardon me for stating the obvious, but there really is no such thing as a virginal motherhood, as it defies all the laws of nature. In effect, it was not possible. Things like this just don't happen. Interestingly enough, however, Gabriel didn't feel the need to elaborate. Instead he went on to explain that the resulting child would be the Son of God. Incredibly, that was all he said about the topic. I invite you to pause for a minute and think about what Mary has just been told. Think about what would be going through your mind, especially after hearing Gabriel's answer. I don't think any of us would fault Mary for asking more questions or for flat-out saying, "I'm sorry, Gabriel, but I think you may have the wrong person for the job." Mary, however, remained silent and let the angel finish what he had to say. Although there is no indication that Mary expressed any doubt or asked for a sign, Gabriel left her with some additional information: "Elizabeth, your relative, has also conceived a son in her old age, and this is the sixth month for her who was called barren; for nothing will be impossible for God" (Luke 1:36–37).

What was the significance of this additional piece of information? These words must have been important or Gabriel wouldn't have spoken the words and, more importantly, they wouldn't be recorded in the Bible. I also believe that part of the message is directed more toward us than it was toward Mary. Our Lady was informed that her elderly relative Elizabeth was now six months pregnant. Soon after hearing the news, Mary would journey to the hill country to offer her assistance. This information was important to her, and she acted upon it. On the other hand, the final part of the message is something Mary knew very well. If Mary didn't question how a virginal conception would take place by the power of the Holy Spirit, she obviously knew that nothing will be impossible with God. However, countless generations needed and will need to hear Gabriel's parting words: "For nothing will be impossible with God." A virginal motherhood, a healing from cancer, finding a job after receiving hundreds of rejection letters, a solution to an "impossible" problem: Gabriel provides us with the answer and a reason to hope.

After hearing all the angel had to say, Mary will make a statement summing up how she views herself and how she views her relationship with God. Although they are familiar to most of us, our Lady's simple words warrant a closer look. This statement contains a veritable encyclopedia of information about how she viewed herself and her relationship with God: "Behold, I am the handmaid of the Lord. May it be done to me according to your word" (Luke 1:38).

The dictionary says a handmaid is essentially a servant. Someone who fulfills this role doesn't pick and choose which of her assigned duties will get carried out. If a handmaid is given something to do, she does it. No negotiation, no questions, no objections. In fact, a handmaid carries out her duties without expecting a reward. In today's society, we understandably have a hard time accepting this kind of a role. We may even look at Mary's comment and feel sorry for her. Shouldn't she be able to object or have a say in what God asks her to do? Doesn't she have rights? What's really remarkable and beautiful about Mary's proclamation is she freely chose to use those words.

Gabriel didn't ask her to become the Lord's servant. Instead he came with a specific task in mind and asked for her consent. Loving God as she did, however, Mary's answer far surpassed what was required. She was not content with saying "yes" to this one request, but she wanted to assent to everything the Lord would ask of her, now and in the future.

Why was Mary able to make this unqualified statement? Because she loved God and because she was humble. Humility is not something that comes easy to many of us. We view certain tasks and jobs as being beneath us. On the other hand, Mary understood and embraced her role as God's handmaid. She made her proclamation without any qualifications whatsoever. She was the Lord's servant in all circumstances, not just the favorable ones. The details didn't really matter to her. What was important was that she was willing to do anything God asked of her. That's exactly what a good and faithful servant does.

Mary's humility reminds us of how Jesus lived his life. Although he was God, our Lord humbled himself and took the form of a slave (Philippians 2:6–8), becoming man so you and I could one day go to heaven. Fortunately for us, Jesus didn't feel it was beneath him to become one of us. He voluntarily subjected himself to a life of humiliation and suffering so we would one day be able to live with him in paradise. Instead of having the Apostles wash his feet, Jesus washed their feet (John 13:3–15). He came not to be served but to serve others (Matthew 20:28). That is exactly how Mary viewed her relationship with God and with those around her.

Despite the fact that she was conceived without the stain of original sin and was chosen to be the Mother of the Savior, Mary didn't view herself as a privileged character but rather as a humble servant.

How important is it that we emulate Mary's humility? The Bible tells us that, without humility, it is impossible for us to enter the kingdom of heaven (Psalm 18:27, Job 22:29, Mark 10:15). Although extremely important, humility is one of the most difficult virtues to acquire. When we read St. Paul's instruction to "regard others as better than yourselves," we cringe and automatically think of all of those people who are *not* better than us. Completely ignoring the fact that we can't judge anyone's motives, we're quick to condemn others for their faults and claim "they knew what they were doing" and accuse them of dishonesty.

In addition to struggling to practice humility with others, we sometimes even fail to be humble with the Lord. As evidence, look at how many times we question events that occur in our lives. Why is God allowing this to happen to me? We pray "thy will be done" and, at the same time, provide the Lord with a list of acceptable answers to our prayers. Some even go as far as to disobey teachings of the Church because they don't agree with them. We lash out at God when things don't go our way. These positions are all incompatible with the virtue of humility and illustrate a serious misunderstanding of who's the Creator and who's the creature. If we are truly willing to live out God's will in our lives, then we should be willing to accept his answers, even when they conflict with our wants.

So how can we handle this lack of humility that creeps into all of our lives at some point? The first thing we can do is to meditate on our Lady's words to the angel. She proclaimed her willingness to be God's servant, now and in the future. Her humility brings more glory to the Lord than a thousand works done out of pride. It didn't matter to Mary what God asked of her. All that mattered was that she was doing his will. There will be times when we feel like giving the Lord a list of ways in which we're willing to serve him. There are certain things we just don't want to do, thinking they're too difficult or beneath us. Mary gave the Lord no such limitations. Whatever he asked, she'd be willing to do. Ask her to help you make the same offer to God. Once the limitations are removed, you'll be amazed at what he'll do in your life.

The Message: Be willing to serve God according to his wishes, not your own. A true servant doesn't complain about doing his master's will, even if it involves suffering and inconvenience.

Reflection Questions

1. Are you willing to proclaim, like Mary, that you are the Lord's servant? Are you willing to do anything that God asks of you in the future, even if you don't know the details?

2. Think of a situation that required you to practice humility. How did it feel?

3. Recall that Jesus was born in a stable and lived a life of poverty. Do you view certain situations or occupations as being beneath you? If so, why?

4. Do you complain about unpleasant events that occur in your life? If so, what does that say about your relationship with God?

5. What do you think of when you hear the word "handmaid" or "servant?" Would you like to become the Lord's servant, even if it involves unpleasant duties?

CHAPTER 3

Thy Will Be Done

"May it be done to me according to your word."

LUKE 1:38

It's pretty obvious that anyone who declares herself to be "the handmaid of the Lord" wouldn't have a problem with any assignment God sends her way. That is, provided she's being sincere. We all know the routine. "Anything you want, Lord. I'll do whatever you want...just say the word." How many times do we profess our desire to do God's will only to change our minds when the going gets tough? Even though we're sincere at the time, we often change our tune once we realize what we've gotten ourselves into. Mary, on the other hand, really meant what she said, a fact that can be supported by looking at how she lived her life. Having first proclaimed her general desire to be God's servant, our Lady then backed up her promise with a specific answer to the angel's request. As would be expected, she gave her full consent.

So why was Mary able to make this definitive commitment while we fail so many times? Much of it has to do with the fact that we're a lot like babies. I know it's painful to hear, but it's true. Infants are known for being self-centered. A baby doesn't care who he's inconveniencing when he wants to eat. All he knows is that he's hungry and is going to cry until he gets what he wants. The fact that his mother or father is exhausted doesn't come into play at all. Obviously, babies don't know any better.

17

Some of us, unfortunately, don't outgrow this trait even when we become adults. If we're totally honest with ourselves we'll probably realize that we all fall into this category at times. The basic cause of this phenomenon is that we like to be comfortable. At the risk of oversimplifying the issue, it all boils down to the fact that we're usually happiest when we get what we want.

If we're truly committed to following God's will, however, there will naturally be occasions when we will be required to do things that are not pleasant. Why? Because sometimes what God wants is not what we want. Although this can be a difficult problem to overcome, learning to carry out the Lord's will in all circumstances is the highest form of love we can show him. Sometimes this will require us to make a decision, and sometimes it will involve accepting difficulties that arise unexpectedly. In either case, however, we are given the option to embrace or reject God's will.

Need an example? If we study the life of Christ, we'll get some great advice for dealing with situations in our lives. The familiar acronym WWJD (What Would Jesus Do?) reminds us our actions should always mirror those of the Lord. A good rule of thumb when facing a moral decision is to choose the course of action that Jesus would choose. Fortunately for us, the Gospels contain numerous examples of how Jesus behaved in different situations. One of the greatest examples of choosing God's will even when it was painful can be seen as Jesus prayed in the Garden of Gethsemane on the night before he died:

> "Then Jesus came with them to a place called Gethsemane, and he said to his disciples, 'Sit here while I go over there and pray.' He took along Peter and the two sons of Zebedee, and began to feel sorrow and distress. Then he said to

them, 'My soul is sorrowful even to death. Remain here and keep watch with me.' He advanced a little and fell prostrate in prayer, saying, 'My Father, if it is possible, let this cup pass from me; yet, not as I will, but as you will'" (Matthew 26:36–39).

By praying in this manner, the Lord showed us that sometimes God will ask us to do things that are painful. Learning to submit to his will is the first step on the road to sanctity. As we rely less and less on our feelings when making moral decisions, we'll be able to better discern God's will. Due to our fallen human nature, however, this is sometimes a difficult process. St. Ignatius of Loyola understood this and incorporated suggestions for following these guidelines into his Spiritual Exercises. He constantly drove home the point that our decisions should not be based on what feels good but on what would give the greatest glory to God.

After hearing the details that were explained to the Blessed Mother, most of us would have many more questions and would be begging the angel to stick around. Mary, on the other hand, heard all she needed to hear and was fully prepared to give her answer. If God's messenger said this was the plan, then it was good enough for her. Contrasting Mary's faith with my own faith is painful but enlightening. Hardly a day goes by when I don't question the Lord's ability to resolve some crisis in my life or to give me the grace to endure the resulting suffering. Although the angel's words ("nothing will be impossible for God") are right there in Scripture and etched in my memory, I sometimes fail to believe them. Knowing God can do all things, Mary didn't care that the world would view this as an impossible plan. She knew that with God, all things are possible!

As long as I'm comparing Mary with myself, there's another very big difference in how she handled this situation and how I would probably handle it. Mary didn't even flinch at the fact that her pregnancy is going to be really difficult to explain to Joseph, her family, and to just about all of her other relatives and friends. That's because she loved God with all of her heart and *truly* was his servant. The fact that she was going to be inconvenienced didn't matter to her. She meant what she just said about being the Lord's handmaid. If he wanted her to do something, she would do it with no questions asked. Is anyone else feeling inadequate right now?

Every time we pray the words of the Our Father, we say, "thy will be done," but do we really mean it? Probably...until we run into serious illness, financial difficulties, or the unexpected death of a family member. When faced with problems, our desire to do God's will often goes out the window. Each day, you and I are given the opportunity to say "yes" to God. Like Mary, we are often asked to submit to his will without knowing all the details. Whether it's being open to having additional children, pursuing a religious vocation, or contributing more to charitable causes, the Lord often requests our consent. Are we so concerned about the details or potential difficulties that we say, "no thanks?" Or, like the Blessed Mother, do we declare ourselves to be the Lord's servants, trusting in his providence? If we are able to turn our lives over to the Lord and let him use us as he sees fit, there's no telling how much good he can accomplish through us. Despite the fact that we are frail and weak, the Lord can and will use us to do great things. Oftentimes we are afraid to imitate Mary and commit our lives fully to God, fearing that we won't be strong enough to deal with the difficulties that may arise. St. Paul reminds us that these fears are pointless, for God's grace is all we need. As the Apostle himself stated, "for when I am weak, then I am strong" (2 Corinthians 12:10).

Imagine for a minute that the Lord asked you to carry a very heavy cross. He sent an angel and relayed the message that you've been chosen to contract a very serious form of cancer that would involve much suffering. By carrying your cross, you'll be able to inspire and help many other cancer patients, many of whom have no hope. You won't know exactly how bad your suffering will be, how long it will last, or whether the cancer would prove to be fatal. As you mull over the positives, you realize that your patient suffering would help many others. On the other hand, you're not sure how painful this is going to be and if you'll be able to endure the suffering. How would you respond? Would you say, "yes," "no," or, "It depends...I need more details?"

While discerning God's will often requires prayer and meditation, sometimes it's *a lot* easier to discover. By simply accepting those things that happen to us on a daily basis (at our jobs, in our families, when we become ill), we are saying "yes" to God and following his will. When unpleasant or painful events occur in our lives, we can complain or we can echo the words of our Blessed Mother: "May it be done to me according to your word."

Although Mary didn't refuse God's request, she understands the temptation to do so. She undoubtedly experienced confusion throughout her life and needed to ponder things in her heart (Luke 2:19). The Blessed Mother knows we are sometimes scared and confused and wants to help. She also knows the good that can result when one says "yes" to the Lord. Ask her for the grace to be able to do God's will even when it's painful. She's been there, she's experienced tough times, and she will help.

The Message: God loves us so much that he gives us the gift of free will. When he asks me to do something, I can say "yes" or "no." Mary said, "yes." How about me?

Reflection Questions

1. Recall some situations when you chose to do what others wished instead of what you wished. How did you feel afterward?

2. After the angel finished speaking to Mary, the Bible tells us he departed. How do you think Mary felt after the angel left? Picture yourself in her situation. How would you feel?

3. How often do you make decisions based on what feels good instead of basing your choice on what God wants?

4. Read the account of Jesus' agony in the Garden (Matthew 26:36–46). What can we learn from the way he prayed?

5. Are you afraid to say, "thy will be done" to God for the rest of your life, even though it may involve suffering? If so, what is it that frightens you the most and why?

CHAPTER 4

Singing God's Praise

"My soul proclaims the greatness of the Lord;
my spirit rejoices in God my savior."

LUKE 1:46–47

Consider for a moment what's happening in Mary's life. She is engaged to be married and has just conceived a child while remaining a virgin. Oh, I almost forgot, that child will be the long-awaited Messiah! Although it's just about impossible to fully comprehend what she was going through, it's worthwhile that we think about the details for a minute. Mary and Joseph were engaged to be married and there were things that needed to get done. After Eileen and I became engaged, we were very busy for several months. We had to find a caterer, hire a photographer, make arrangements for the church, choose the invitations, find a band for the reception, meet with the priest, etc. Although it was a busy time, it was also an exciting time. We imagined where we would live, how many children we'd have, and what our life together would be like. I'm sure Mary had all of the same obligations and dreams as most brides-to-be. Now try to imagine how she must have felt when Gabriel appeared and explained the new details. It makes her "yes" even more impressive, doesn't it? Furthermore, despite her life being completely turned upside down, what did Mary do as soon as the angel departed? She traveled in haste (she was in a hurry) to visit Elizabeth, who was elderly and six months pregnant. Now that's what I call charity!

After Mary arrived and greeted Elizabeth, she was showered with praise by her grateful relative who cried out in a loud voice:

"Most blessed are you among women, and blessed is the fruit of your womb. And how does this happen to me, that the mother of my Lord should come to me? For at the moment the sound of your greeting reached my ears, the infant in my womb leaped for joy. Blessed are you who believed that what was spoken to you by the Lord would be fulfilled" (Luke 1:42–45).

Sounds like Elizabeth was really happy to see Mary, doesn't it? When we read these words, we get an idea of how much Elizabeth admired and respected Mary. Additionally, we see an example of the power of Jesus who, while still in Mary's womb, was able to fill Elizabeth with the Holy Spirit. But since we're focusing on Mary, let's look at her response, as it presents a clear insight as to how she thought and provides us with a powerful message. Her prayerful words, commonly known as the Magnificat, begin as follows: "My soul proclaims the greatness of the Lord."

We've discussed Mary's humility previously, and we can see another example of it here. After hearing all the praises heaped on her by Elizabeth, our Lady turns the attention away from herself and directs it toward God. While Mary's words provide great insight about her personality, they also provide a standard by which to measure our own humility. Most of us like to be praised. We enjoy it when our bosses tell us we're doing a good job or when friends say they admire our faith or compliment the way we look or dress. It feels good, doesn't it? On the other hand, it can be extremely painful when we're criticized or humiliated. Although there's nothing wrong with being praised, we want to make sure that it doesn't become our motivation for doing the right thing. Furthermore, we want to make sure we give credit to God for giving us the grace to be good.

Now, why wouldn't Mary simply thank Elizabeth for her kind words? It would have been a perfectly humble and appropriate response. While we can be certain that our Lady appreciated the compliment, we also know she was very aware of God's presence in her life. Even though she knew she never sinned, Mary understood that her goodness was due to God's grace. When Elizabeth praised her, Mary couldn't help praising God, the source of all of her goodness.

Let's examine our lives for a minute. How much time do we spend praising God for his goodness? Even if we have a good relationship with the Lord, we probably spend most of our prayer time asking him for favors. Certainly there's nothing wrong with that, and Jesus specifically told us if we ask, we'll receive (Matthew 7:7). But as in any relationship, it's important that we don't fall into the trap of constantly asking for things. Imagine how pleased God would be if we came to him seeking nothing but instead offered him praise. So where do we start? I've found that the Psalms are perfect for this type of prayer. Here are a few examples:

"I love you, LORD, my strength,
LORD, my rock, my fortress, my deliverer,
My God, my rock of refuge,
my shield, my saving horn, my stronghold!
Praised be the LORD, I exclaim!
I have been delivered from my enemies" (Psalm 18:2–4).

"You who hear our prayers.
To you all flesh must come
with its burden of wicked deeds.

We are overcome by our sins;
only you can pardon them" (Psalm 65:3–4).

"Sing to God, praise his name;
exalt the rider of the clouds.
Rejoice before him
whose name is the LORD" (Psalm 68:5).

"Bless the LORD, my soul!
LORD, my God, you are great indeed" (Psalm 104:1).

A big part of recognizing the Lord's greatness is reflecting all that he has done for each one of us personally. Many of us are so busy or focus so much on our needs that we neglect to acknowledge the many blessings given to us by God. As we listen to Mary's prayerful words, we can plainly see she's grateful for all the Lord has done for her: "...my spirit rejoices in God my savior."

Rejoice. It's a word that's familiar to us, but how much of our day is actually spent rejoicing? St. Paul tells us that we should "rejoice in the Lord always" (Philippians 4:4). Does that mean we should rejoice even when troubles arise in our lives? Since he said, "always," I guess so. Why should I be joyful if my life is falling apart? Essentially the clue is contained in Mary's proclamation. She is rejoicing when reflecting on her Savior. If we follow her example and call to mind the fact that we were redeemed through the actions of Jesus our Savior, then it becomes possible to rejoice always. For "neither death, nor life, nor angels, nor principalities, nor present things, nor future things, nor powers, nor height, nor depth, nor any other creature will be able to separate us from the love of God in Christ Jesus our Lord" (Romans 8:38–39). If that's the case, then why shouldn't we rejoice?

Given Mary's mindset, we can understand why she has a spirit of joy. What can prove to be very confusing, however, is the fact that she's rejoicing in God her Savior. If Mary was sinless, you may ask, why did she need a Savior? This verse is often used by those seeking to disprove the Catholic dogma of the Immaculate Conception. They contend that Mary couldn't have been conceived without original sin because Mary's own words in the Bible prove she needed a Savior. In reality, Mary's words are true. She *did* need a Savior. She was also conceived without the stain of original sin. In the Apostolic Constitution *Ineffabilis Deus* (December 8, 1854), Pope Pius IX declared that Mary was granted a unique gift and redeemed through the merits of Jesus Christ. Just like all other humans, Mary was in need of redemption and was indeed redeemed. However, unlike the rest of humanity, she was redeemed in advance. Mary's Immaculate Conception is not a fabrication, it does not contradict Scripture, but it represents a unique one-time gift given to the Mother of the Savior.

Ever mindful of the fact that her goodness can be attributed to God, Mary cannot help but rejoice in his magnificence. She is thankful for her redemption and expresses it in her prayer. Are you grateful for the fact that you were redeemed by Jesus? Sometimes we forget there's nothing we could have done to make our redemption possible. That victory was won for us by Jesus more than 2,000 years ago on Calvary. By virtue of his painful sacrifice and subsequent rising from the dead, you and I can now go to heaven. That possibility is 100 percent due to the actions of Christ. We had nothing to do with it. When viewed in that light, it is easier to be grateful, isn't it? Our redemption is a completely unmerited gift. Mary understood that and expressed it. Do we?

The Message: Mary was quick to sing the praises of the Lord and recognize she was greatly blessed. She knew her goodness was due to God's grace. Because we have been blessed with many things, including redemption, our prayers, therefore, should reflect a sense of gratitude for God's kindness.

Reflection Questions

1. What can you learn from Mary's quick response to the needs of Elizabeth? Is there someone in your life who needs your assistance?

2. Have you ever thought you were doing a good job only to be criticized by others? How did it feel? Are your actions sometimes motivated by the praise you hope to receive?

3. Look around at God's creation. Compile a list of things that reflect his greatness.

4. Think of five things in your life that should cause you to rejoice.

5. Mary brought Jesus to Elizabeth. Name some ways you can bring him to those around you.

CHAPTER 5

Blessed By God

"For he has looked upon his handmaid's lowliness;
behold, from now on will all ages call me blessed.
The Mighty One has done great things for me,
and holy is his name."

<small>LUKE 1:48–49</small>

One of Jesus' recurring messages was that the humble will be rewarded. When the disciples wanted to know who was greatest in the kingdom of heaven, Jesus summoned a child to him and stated: "Whoever humbles himself like this child is the greatest in the kingdom of heaven" (Matthew 18:4).

In a parable designed to emphasize the proper practice of humility (Luke 14:7–11), Jesus uses a wedding feast to teach an important lesson. Anyone listening to this parable in Jesus' day would understand that the seating at a banquet was done according to social status. The place of honor was next to the host, with other esteemed guests seated nearby. When invited to a wedding feast, Jesus stated that one should not choose a seat of honor. Doing so puts one at the risk of being displaced when a guest of greater importance arrives. Instead the Lord recommends that a guest choose the lowest place. This will allow the host to honor his guest by inviting him to move up to a more desired seat. To put it in modern terms, it's similar to a first-class upgrade on an airline. Jesus closes the parable with the words: "For everyone who exalts himself will be humbled, but the one who humbles himself will be exalted" (Luke 14:11).

To put this parable into spiritual terms, those who are humble and recognize their standing before God will one day be rewarded with eternal life in heaven. Those who are proud and constantly seek to call attention to their importance will not. This is a very simple but often disregarded teaching.

The Lord's emphasis on humility wasn't an unfamiliar teaching. The importance of this virtue was addressed throughout the Old Testament as well:

"When pride comes, disgrace comes; but with the humble is wisdom" (Proverbs 11:2).

"For humble people you save; haughty eyes you bring low" (Psalm 18:28).

"For the LORD of hosts will have his day against all that is proud and arrogant, against all that is high, and it will be brought low" (Isaiah 2:12).

Although the virtue of humility is extremely important in the life of a Christian, it is quite often misunderstood. Some incorrectly assume that being humble and having low self-esteem go hand in hand. In addition, it's often thought humility makes it impossible to accept compliments for a job well done. In other words, if someone tells me I have a nice singing voice, I should reply with, "No I don't." In reality, being humble means nothing of the kind. Humility is simply having a true picture of oneself. In addition to looking objectively at our sinfulness, true humility also enables us to recognize our talents. It does not mean denying our God-given gifts but rather recognizing them for what they are: gifts from God. Paul writes of this in his First Letter to the Corinthians: "What do you possess that you have not received? But if you have received it, why are you boasting as if you did not receive it?" (1 Corinthians 4:7).

Instead of denying she was blessed with certain gifts, such as the ability to avoid sin, Mary rejoiced in her lowliness and gave glory to the Lord for the blessings she had received. In doing this, she is giving us a perfect example of how we should treat the gifts we've been given by God. Looking once again at St. Paul's message to the Corinthians, we see further support for Mary's words:

> "Consider your own calling, brothers. Not many of you were wise by human standards, not many were powerful, not many were of noble birth. Rather, God chose the foolish of the world to shame the wise, and God chose the weak of the world to shame the strong, and God chose the lowly and despised of the world, those who count for nothing, to reduce to nothing those who are something, so that no human being might boast before God" (1 Corinthians 1:26–29).

The Lord often chooses those who are considered lowly (in the eyes of the world) to accomplish great things. Mary was a poor virgin from an unimportant town (Nazareth) who was chosen by God to deliver the Messiah to the world. She wasn't chosen because of her superior intelligence, good looks, or because of her worldly success. The reason she was chosen is known to God alone. We do know that once she was chosen, however, she was given all of the grace needed to fulfill her mission. As we meditate upon Mary's words in the Magnificat, we see she wasn't being egotistical about her gifts. Rather, she was acknowledging them and praising God for gracing her with his generosity.

Look around at the people in your life. How many times do we refer to someone as having a special gift? We have all been given talents by God. Some people are great evangelists, others are good listeners, and still others are doers who have the knack for getting things done. When used properly, these gifts complement each other and can be used to advance God's kingdom on earth. To acknowledge these gifts is not to be proud but rather to pay tribute to the Lord's goodness.

Once again, St. Paul explains this concept in his writings to the Church at Corinth:

> "There are different kinds of spiritual gifts but the same Spirit; there are different forms of service but the same Lord; there are different workings but the same God who produces all of them in everyone. To each individual the manifestation of the Spirit is given for some benefit" (1 Corinthians 12:4–7).

Finally, Mary reflects one last time on the Lord's goodness to her, and she does it in her typically humble manner. We can learn much about people by studying their choice of words, and Mary's words are no exception. Referring to God as the "Mighty One" gives us an insightful look as to how she views God. In Mary's eyes, the Lord is mighty and she is a mere creature. While in today's society that may be viewed as a sign of weakness, it's actually a very accurate view of God and his power. Whether we want to admit it or not, the Lord is all-powerful and we are not. Keeping that in mind is very good for our spiritual lives and helps us to see things as they really are.

Mary then closes this section of the Magnificat with a very

meaningful proclamation about the holiness of the Lord. While it is sometimes overlooked, it is one of the most important things she has to say and should be taken very seriously. It is a reminder for those of us who sometimes become lax about how we refer to God. She proclaims: "Holy is his name."

There is no doubt that God is holy. Numerous Scripture references (Leviticus 19:2, Isaiah 6:3, Revelation 4:8) and our own common sense make this fact known. Mary's close relationship with the Lord and her knowledge of Scripture, however, allows her to take it a step further. As detailed many times in the Old Testament (1 Chronicles 16:35, Psalm 30:4), Mary understands that not only is God holy, but his very *name* is holy. That is a profound revelation that we shouldn't take lightly. How many times do we use the Lord's name in vain or use it carelessly? No big deal, you say? It was to the Israelites who, out of respect for God, wouldn't even pronounce his name, using the word "*Adonai*" (Lord, in English) instead. While modern-day Christians don't continue this practice, there should be a respect when using the Lord's name. Mary understood this, and her proclamation should serve as a reminder for us who may become tempted to become too casual about our relationship with God. He certainly wants us to speak to him frequently and desires to be our best friend, but we should never lose sight of the fact that God is Almighty and our Creator. This is the underlying theme that runs throughout Mary's Magnificat.

Mary certainly knew she was blessed. In addition to being conceived without original sin, she was chosen to play an incredible role in salvation history—the Mother of the Savior. Mary understood, however, that these blessings originated from God and were not "earned" by her. She never made the mistake of being overcome by pride. Mary knew her goodness came from God. She also understood his holiness and power. It was because of her understanding that she was able to give him all the credit. We have all been blessed by God in many ways, the most important being our redemption. Let's ask Mary to help us better appreciate the Lord as the source of all these good things.

The Message: God has blessed us with many things. He has given us various talents that can be used to build up his kingdom on earth. He has also given us the ultimate gift of our redemption, which allows us to one day live in heaven. Like Mary, we should be grateful for these gifts and be mindful that they all originate from God's goodness.

Reflection Questions

1. Name some gifts or talents that are present in your own life and in the lives of those around you. How can those gifts be used to bring glory to God?

2. Has anyone ever told you that you had a gift? How did you reply?

3. Over the course of your life, were you surprised to discover you had some previously unknown gifts? How did you discover them?

4. Is there anything you feel called to do (becoming a religious-education teacher, volunteer at a nursing home, etc.) but don't have the confidence to carry it out? Could this be a hidden gift?

5. Call to mind some of the blessings you've received in your life. Compose a brief prayer to thank God for them.

CHAPTER 6

God's Mercy

"His mercy is from age to age to those who fear him."

LUKE 1:50

At first glance, it appears that Mary's words are a little restrictive. Is she really saying that God will only be merciful to those who fear him? Without some background information, this statement can be very confusing and downright scary. In order to understand what she is saying, let's first discuss *fear of the Lord*. The whole idea of fearing God has become very unpopular in the present age, and we've moved toward a kinder, gentler version of the Lord. Unfortunately, that shift in thinking has created many problems in the world and often causes us to believe that sin is no big deal anymore because we're dealing with a warm and fuzzy God who really doesn't care if we disobey his commands. While it's true that the Lord will continue to love us no matter how much we sin, there's a little more to it than that.

Let's first look at what the Bible says about fear of the Lord. Throughout the pages of Scripture, there are many references to this kind of fear. And rather than it being discouraged, fear of the Lord is always encouraged.

"The LORD your God, shall you fear; him shall you serve, and by his name shall you swear" (Deuteronomy 6:13).

"But you must fear the LORD and serve him faithfully with all your heart, for you have seen the great things the LORD has done among you" (1 Samuel 12:24).

"The fear of the LORD is the beginning of wisdom; prudent are all who practice it" (Psalm 111:10).

"I shall show you whom to fear. Be afraid of the one who after killing has the power to cast into Gehenna; yes, I tell you, be afraid of that one" (Luke 12:5).

So what exactly is fear of the Lord and why is it a good thing? Before I delve into that topic I want to first make the point that *fear of the Lord* takes on different shapes. While there are varying degrees of this kind of fear, let's examine the two ends of the spectrum. Although both types of Godly fear are good (because they keep us out of trouble), one is definitely more noble than the other. The most basic and primitive form of fear of the Lord is known as *servile* fear. Basically this is the fear of getting in trouble. In a worldly sense, this is what stops you from doing 80 MPH in a 35 MPH zone or what makes you stop browsing the Internet when your boss comes to your desk.

Turning our thoughts to God, at some point in our lives we've all experienced that feeling of "if I commit this sin I'm going to have to answer for it one day." Despite our lack of pure intentions, this kind of fear serves a purpose and is often sufficient to keep us out of hell. Rather than feeling bad about this less-than-perfect kind of fear, I'm thankful for experiencing it many times in my life. Our fallen human nature often causes us to seek pleasure over doing the right thing. When this happens, a good dose of servile fear (and its reminder of the consequences of sin) can often stop us from committing a serious sin. Again, it may not be perfect, but it sure beats eternal damnation. In addition, this form of fear is often the first step to a greater and more loving relationship with the Lord. For many of us, it was our initial attempt at getting closer to God.

On the other hand, the purest form of fear of the Lord is known as *filial* fear. This occurs when you love God so much that you fear separation from him through sin. With this type of fear, it's really sin (and not God) that scares you. I can offer a simplified example of this from my childhood. When I got in trouble (and it didn't happen much...really), my biggest concern was that I let my parents down. The fact that I would be punished was secondary. I loved my mom and dad and I always wanted to do the right thing. And I didn't want to hurt them by doing something that would make them sad. Having this type of feeling about offending God would be an example of filial fear of the Lord. Many of you will recall that fear of the Lord is one of the seven gifts of the Holy Spirit. It is not servile fear but filial fear that is considered to be a gift of the Holy Spirit. Although it may still be in seed form (and remain somewhat undeveloped), those of us who have been baptized and confirmed have some degree of this gift present inside of us. Although St. Thomas Aquinas considered fear of the Lord to be the least of the gifts (wisdom is the highest), he emphasized that all of the Holy Spirit's gifts are necessary for salvation. Therefore, we should be thankful for this gift and continually pray for an increase in it and all of the gifts.

Now let's get back to Mary's proclamation that God has mercy on those who fear him. When we look at the concept of mercy, it's a given that the one who is able to show mercy is in a position of authority over the one who will receive mercy. This is hardly a news flash, but God is greater than us. He doesn't *have* to show mercy, but he does because he's all loving. If there's one weakness that many of us have (and I count myself in this category), it's an underappreciation of God's mercy. It's way too easy to forget that we don't deserve to live in heaven. Every day we commit numerous offenses against God. Some of these can be very serious. In the *Catechism of the Catholic Church*, the Church teaches that we (sinners) are the ones who are ultimately responsible for the crucifixion of Christ (*CCC* 598). But in his mercy, God not only offers to forgive our sins through the sacrament of reconciliation but grants us the opportunity to one day live with him in heaven. In his Letter to Titus, St. Paul sums up the situation nicely:

> "For we ourselves were once foolish, disobedient, deluded, slaves to various desires and pleasures, living in malice and envy, hateful ourselves and hating one another. But when the kindness and generous love of God our savior appeared, not because of any righteous deeds we had done but because of his mercy, he saved us through the bath of rebirth and renewal by the holy Spirit, whom he richly poured out on us through Jesus Christ our savior, so that we might be justified by his grace and become heirs in hope of eternal life" (Titus 3:3–7).

This is exactly the point Mary is trying to make. None of us deserves to live forever with the Lord in eternal happiness. At some point (maybe every day), we can all identify with one or more of the items on St. Paul's aforementioned list of bad qualities. In his mercy, however, Jesus Christ pours out his graces on us and makes it possible for us to achieve our salvation. Best of all, as pointed out by Mary, this will continue from age to age. It's not as if those who lived during the Lord's time were the only ones who could benefit. This offer will last until the end of time. What's the catch, you ask? Mary explains what is necessary to take advantage of the Lord's offer. It is for all those who fear the Lord. Whether it's servile or filial fear isn't really as important as the end result—that we obey his commands. While we should certainly strive to obey solely out of love, obeying out of fear in many cases is a step in the right direction. If we take our Lady's words to heart and try our best to love and please God, we will receive his mercy.

The Message: Through the ages and for all generations to come, God will be merciful to those who love him.

Reflection Questions

1. What are some ways the Lord has been merciful to you?
2. Try to recall some occasions when fear of the Lord helped you to avoid sin. How about after committing the sin? Did fear of the Lord ever cause you to repent and seek God's forgiveness?
3. How can you show mercy to those in your life? Be specific.
4. In your life, are you motivated more by servile or filial fear of the Lord?
5. Think about those times when others have shown mercy to you. How did it feel? Does recalling these occurrences help you to show mercy to others?

CHAPTER 7

The Last Shall Be First

"He has shown might with his arm,
dispersed the arrogant of mind and heart.
He has thrown down the rulers from their thrones
but lifted up the lowly.
The hungry he has filled with good things;
the rich he has sent away empty."

LUKE 1:51–53

In the beginning of Mary's Magnificat, she spoke about the greatness of God and how he has blessed her. She then proceeded to discuss the Lord's mercy and how he has and will continue to show mercy to those who love him. As her prayer nears its end, Mary now takes a look back in time and reflects on how the Lord rewards the lowly and punishes the proud. Far from being a history lesson, Mary's words contain an important message for each of us.

When I was young, I was very shy and wasn't especially popular. Although I was so quiet that I wasn't usually picked on by the bullies, I was still very much afraid of them. While I'm not revealing names (they might come looking for me), I do remember several kids who could definitely be classified as bullies. They were generally big and loud, and they would boss others around and wouldn't hesitate to use physical violence if they didn't get their way. I have to admit that it made me happy when these troublemakers would get caught in the act by the teacher. I can't lie: It did feel good to see them get in trouble, but seeing them get punished wasn't the main reason for my joy. My happiness was due to the fact that I now felt safe to know that I had a protector (the teacher) to watch over me and the other "helpless" victims of the bullies. We couldn't defend ourselves against the power of these young tyrants, but we had someone who was able to do it for us. Although this example is somewhat simplified, it does shed light on how the Lord works. Putting it into plain English, anyone who wants to be a bully and abuse his power must one day answer to God. It may not happen in this life, but it will happen in the next. On the other hand, as Mary states, the humble will be rewarded.

Let's be clear about one thing. This message is a lot more complicated than saying, "God will punish the arrogant." Although that's basically true, Mary's observation serves not only as an after-the-fact reflection but also as a rule by which to live one's life. It reminds us of a fact of which Mary was well aware: Without God we are nothing. If we forget that fact and begin to rely solely on our own abilities, then we'll be in for a rude awakening. That's exactly the mistake the schoolyard bullies in my past made, and it's the mistake made by people who think they don't need God.

Several years after Mary spoke these words, St. Paul addressed the topic in his First Letter to the Church at Corinth:

> "Rather, God chose the foolish of the world to shame the wise, and God chose the weak of the world to shame the strong, and God chose the lowly and despised of the world, those who count for nothing, to reduce to nothing those who are something..." (1 Corinthians 1:27–28).

And why was that?

"...So that no human being might boast before God" (1 Corinthians 1:29).

Let's pause for a minute and reflect on the meaning of Mary's words. Is she saying that God has something against the rulers and the rich? Not at all. As is often the case with biblical verses, we need to dig a little deeper in order to extract the true meaning. Rather than being a blanket condemnation for all who are wealthy or in a position of authority, we can obtain a twofold meaning from her words.

Our Lady's statement can first be taken as words of encouragement for the poor and powerless. In her time, as in the present day, there is a perception (sadly, a pretty accurate one) that money means power. The rich can seemingly do anything they want. If you have enough money, you can get the best medical treatment, escape from legal trouble, and live a very comfortable life. The media feed on this by showcasing the homes and lifestyles of the rich and famous. As a result, many "ordinary" people spend hours dreaming of how much better their lives would be if they were wealthy. While this is not the case at all, it's hard to explain that to someone who is working three jobs just to pay the rent.

Mary understood this, and her words can serve as a source of comfort to those of us who are not wealthy. All are welcome in God's kingdom—the poor as well as the rich. There are no dues, no admission fee, and no credit checks. We are all equal in the Lord's eyes, and Mary is an example of this. She was poor, unknown, and came from an unimportant town, and yet she was chosen to become the Mother of God. She understood this concept completely and wants to offer a word of hope to those the world considers poor or lowly. We are every bit as important to God as the multi-billionaire who lives in a palatial mansion. Anyone who seeks the Lord's assistance, rich or poor, will receive it. There is no admission fee for the kingdom of God, and this is emphasized by the prophet Isaiah in the Old Testament: "All you who are thirsty, come to the water! You who have no money, come, buy grain and eat; Come, buy grain without money, wine and milk without cost" (Isaiah 55:1).

In addition to building up the hope of the poor, Mary's words contain a warning to those who are rich: Excessive wealth can make it difficult to get to heaven. Not that it will make it impossible, but it can become an obstacle. This is a message that is reinforced many times in the pages of the Bible. In his encounter with the rich young man (Luke 18:18–30), Jesus had a strong warning for the rich when he said: "How hard it is for those who have wealth to enter the kingdom of God?" (Luke 18:24). Then after one of his stunned listeners asked who can be saved, the Lord qualified the statement with the words: "What is impossible for human beings is possible for God" (Luke 18:27).

Wealth, in and of itself, does not prevent one from getting to heaven. Although it can present a challenge, it does not exclude one from the kingdom. The key lies in our attitude. St. Paul drives this notion home by making an important point. Often mis-quoted, this statement sums up how wealth can be our downfall: "For the love of money is the root of all evils" (1 Timothy 6:10).

Note, he never said *money* is the root of all evils, but rather, the *love of* money! That makes all the difference in the world, and that is the point Mary is trying to make when she said the rich will be sent away empty. If we seek our comfort in money and material possessions, there will be no room in our lives for God.

So what's the solution for the wealthy? Must they give away all of their wealth in order to get to heaven? That hardly seems realistic or fair. The answer to this question can be found by looking at the first beatitude: "Blessed are the poor in spirit, for theirs is the kingdom of heaven" (Matthew 5:3).

Jesus is stressing the importance of spiritual poverty. This virtue can be possessed even if one is wealthy. Conversely, there's no guarantee that everyone living in poverty automatically will possess it. Spiritual poverty is a state of mind that allows you to be detached from your possessions and rely on God. When practicing it, you realize that everything you've been given (including your talents) comes from the Lord. Therefore, you're not overly concerned about accumulating wealth or holding on to your possessions. As a result, gathering as many possessions as possible isn't your primary goal in life, and you share what you have (both possessions and time) with others. If you experience loss of material goods or even of your health, you don't feel like it's the end of the world. Instead you accept the loss as being part of God's plan for your life.

While this way of thinking does not come naturally to us, it is possible to achieve with God's grace. We can also turn to our Lady and ask for her intercession. The fact that she used these words lets us know she understands them. Mary can help us obtain the graces we need to seek out spiritual wealth and to recall our need for God. Those who ignore this and make it a priority to obtain power and wealth in this life have already received their reward. There is no room in their lives for God's blessings. If we empty ourselves and approach the Lord as a beggar, however, we can look forward to receiving our true reward in heaven.

The Message: In order to receive the spiritual treasures God has planned for us, we must stop focusing solely on earthly possessions. Those who ignore this fact are putting their salvation in jeopardy.

Reflection Questions

1. Discuss ways in which being wealthy can make it difficult to trust in God's providence.

2. Have you ever struggled financially? How was your relationship with the Lord during those times?

3. If you or someone you know is wealthy, what is his secret to remaining close to God?

4. Why do you think the Lord appears to reward some powerful and wealthy people who don't live their lives according to Christian principles? Doesn't this go against what Mary is saying?

5. When you read Mary's words about God filling up the hungry and sending the rich away empty, how do you feel? Does it motivate you to make any changes in your life?

CHAPTER 8

Learning From the Past

"He has helped Israel his servant, remembering his
mercy, according to his promise to our fathers,
to Abraham and to his descendants forever."

Luke 1:54–55

Before becoming a full-time Catholic evangelist, my entire professional career was spent working as a computer programmer and project manager. For thirty years I worked as part of a team. In my earlier years I was a team member and later on I got to manage the team. In both cases, the process was basically the same. A project was assigned to a manager and a team of workers (in my case, computer programmers) was assembled to complete the project. In the companies for which I worked, one thing was constant—the team members would always be changing. Depending on the availability of the programmers, you could be working with a different team for each new project. One lesson I learned quickly was that not all computer programmers are created equal. Some are very productive and always find a way to get the job done on time and others don't. Whether you're a team member or a team manager, knowing the strengths and weaknesses of your team is critical. Decisions often have to be made based upon who's on the team. And how do we evaluate the reliability of the team members? Generally this was accomplished by looking at past performance. While it's not foolproof, one can get a good idea of how well an individual will function on a project by looking at how well he or she functioned on previous assignments.

In life, many people believe we shouldn't look back but instead focus on the present (or the future). While that's somewhat true, we can gain a lot of useful information by examining the past. Certainly corporations believe this or there would be no need to submit a résumé when applying for a job. Hiring executives want to know where you've been and what you've accomplished. If you're choosing a marriage partner, you may decide to pass on someone who has been divorced five times or has been convicted of spousal abuse. While there are always exceptions and people can change, you can get a pretty good picture of someone by looking at his or her past behavior and accomplishments.

Though most of us claim to trust God, our desire can change in a hurry when a crisis occurs in our life. Fortunately, we only need to open our Bible to find documented proof that God does indeed keep his promises. In a world full of uncertainty, this should bring us great comfort. As an example, when Adam and Eve disobeyed and ate the forbidden fruit, God promised that a Savior would be sent to repair the rift caused by their sin: "I will put enmity between you and the woman, and between your offspring and hers; They will strike at your head, while you strike at their heel" (Genesis 3:15).

As promised, the Messiah was born, died, and rose from the dead to redeem a fallen world. Although it took several thousand years, God delivered on his promise. Another example of the Lord's reliability can be seen by looking at the life of Abram (a.k.a. Abraham). Despite having no children and an elderly wife, Abram was promised that his descendants would be as numerous as the stars (Genesis 15:5) and that he would be the father of many nations (Genesis 17:4). And that's exactly what happened. If you read through the Bible, you'll find many examples of the Lord being true to his word. On the other hand, no matter how hard you search, you won't come across a single example where God didn't follow through on his promises. Scripture tells us that even if we are unfaithful to God, he'll still remain faithful (2 Timothy 2:13). Therefore, when Mary highlights God's faithfulness, it's a lot more than just a history lesson. It's a strong reminder that he *always* keeps his promises.

While that's all well and good, what does it mean to us today? For one thing it allows us to take comfort in the fact that if the Lord says something, we can "take it to the bank." As can be seen by looking back at the course of salvation history, his promises are definitely reliable and can be trusted. As we examine our own lives and our own problems, God's trustworthiness becomes extremely pertinent, especially when one considers some of his promises. While keeping in mind all of your problems, take a look at these direct quotes from Jesus:

"Ask and it will be given to you; seek and you will find; knock and the door will be opened to you. For everyone who asks, receives; and the one who seeks, finds; and to the one who knocks, the door will be opened" (Matthew 7:7–8).

"Everything is possible to one who has faith" (Mark 9:23).

"Blessed are you who are now hungry, for you will be satisfied. Blessed are you who are now weeping, for you will laugh" (Luke 6:21).

"For this is the will of my Father, that everyone who sees the Son and believes in him may have eternal life, and I shall raise him [on] the last day" (John 6:40).

"In my Father's house there are many dwelling places. If there were not, would I have told you that I am going to prepare a place for you? And if I go and prepare a place for you, I will come back again and take you to myself, so that where I am you also may be" (John 14:2–3).

Sounds promising, doesn't it? And looking at his history of reliability makes these words sound even more encouraging. Over and over again, we can see that the Lord came through for the Israelites. Therefore, why should we doubt that he'll follow through in our lives? As our Blessed Mother reminds us with her words about Israel, God has always been there for his people. When we look at these events, we can then confidently expect him to keep the promises made to us.

Another effective application of Mary's words can be seen when we look back at our own lives. As we review all of the "impossible" problems and "devastating" crises that we've encountered, what can we conclude? For one thing, if we're able to look back, then it follows that we're still here. All of those disasters that threatened to ruin us not only failed to deliver but, most of the time, never even occurred. Therefore, when we examine our own history, we can see evidence of God's providence in our lives. This is a powerful reminder that he's right there with us. Connecting the dots for a minute, if God always keeps his promises (as can be seen by looking back at salvation history), if he's been there for us in the past (as can be seen by looking back at our past), what does that imply for our future? At the risk of stating the obvious, it reassures us that he's going to be right by our side as we face an unknown future. I don't know about you, but that makes me feel *very* good.

Far from being backward thinking or being stuck in the past, our Lady reminds us that prayerful reflection on the past will remind us of God's loving providence. When we reflect on the many times he helped his people in the past, our confidence in him will grow. In a world that is increasingly cynical and secular, this type of recollection will aid us in believing that he can still part the Red Sea or heal the sick. By carefully examining our own history, we should be able to see many occasions when the Lord came to our rescue. The end result is that our faith will grow stronger and we'll be able to face the future unafraid, knowing we'll never walk alone.

The Message: God has always been there for his people, even when they deserted him. In the same way, God will always be by our side, willing to help us navigate the twists and turns of life.

Reflection Questions

1. What have you learned from your past difficulties and fears? Have these events increased your faith?

2. Name some frightening situations in your past that have turned out well. Offer a brief prayer thanking God for his help.

3. Can you think of some reasons why it's important to know Bible history? How can knowing it help you deal with your problems?

4. When is looking at the past not helpful spiritually? How can you tell when you should and when you shouldn't reflect on past events in your life?

5. God told Abraham to leave his home and his country (Genesis 12:1), and he obeyed. How was this similar to Mary's call in Luke 1:26–38?

CHAPTER 9

Looking for Answers

"Son, why have you done this to us?"

LUKE 2:48

Most of us are familiar with the details of the Finding in the Temple, as detailed in Luke's Gospel (Luke 2:41–52). Each year, Mary and Joseph made the annual trek to Jerusalem for the feast of Passover. Since Jesus was now twelve years old, he was required to make the trip with his parents. On the way home, Mary and Joseph realized Jesus was not with them. They ventured back to Jerusalem and found him in the Temple, instructing the teachers. Great story, everyone is happy, let's move on the next story, right? Unfortunately, this is the way most of us look at this saga. That's a big mistake because there is a lot more to this episode than meets the eye. If we take the time to look into what happened and what was said, we can learn a great deal about Mary and, ultimately, grow in our own relationship with Jesus.

The first thing we should notice is it took three days for Mary and Joseph to find Jesus...*three days!* Those of us who are parents know the horrible feeling that occurs when you can't find your child. A few years ago, my family and I went to our nephew's wedding in Cape May, New Jersey. The reception was at Congress Hall, a very old and elegant hotel. My daughters, Mary and Elizabeth, were nine at the time, and the cocktail hour was extremely crowded. There were so many people standing around that it was hard to see everyone. Eileen and I were getting the chance to catch up with many relatives we hadn't seen in a long time. The girls were playing with their cousins and, even though I have a tendency to be overly protective (boy, is that an understatement), I agreed with Eileen that it would be good for them to be apart from us for a while. Since we were in an unfamiliar setting and the crowd was large, I managed to check on the girls from a distance every now and then. On one of my undercover scouting expeditions, I noticed that Elizabeth was not with the other kids. After fighting my way through the massive crowd, I approached the children and asked about my missing daughter. As is usually the case with kids, no one knew anything. Panic time! Trying my best to avoid looking like a total lunatic, I made my way back to Eileen and informed her that Elizabeth was missing. Together we began searching for her. After scouring the area in vain (the cocktail hour was in the outdoor patio area), we frantically took our search indoors. By this time, my mind was replaying every missing child scenario I'd read about over the course of my lifetime. After what seemed like hours (it was probably close to ten minutes), we located Elizabeth walking up and down one of the hotel corridors, looking in the windows of the little shops. When I asked her what she was doing, she calmly replied that she decided to take a walk. As my heart rate started to return to normal, we all went back to the cocktail hour. Can you imagine how Mary must have felt when Jesus was missing not for three minutes or three hours, but for three whole days? One thing that can be said with certainty is that being the Mother of God didn't come with immunity from anxiety. This episode illustrates that, like us, Mary knew what it was like to walk in darkness at times.

Although it's hard for us to understand how Mary and Joseph

managed to leave Jerusalem without Jesus, understanding the traveling customs of the time helps shed light on the situation. In these times, men and women traveled in separate caravans. As a result, it's totally understandable to see how Mary and Joseph could have thought Jesus was with the other parent. Whatever the reason, however, it's apparent this was a difficult three days for Mary and Joseph. In fact, the loss of the Child Jesus is recognized as one of Mary's Seven Sorrows, a devotion popularized by the Servite order.

While there is a temptation to summarize this saga by stating "all's well that ends well," there are some important details that need to be looked at more closely. Since this is a book about Mary's words, it would make sense that we look at our Lady's first words to Jesus after searching for him for three days: "Son, why have you done this to us?" (Luke 2:48).

Certainly a reasonable question, don't you think? It's a question that any of us who are in her situation can see ourselves asking (although maybe not as eloquently). In fact, it's such a normal question that our natural tendency is to overlook its profundity. We can learn a lot about Mary by carefully observing her words. For one thing, did you notice that our Lady is not only concerned about herself but also about Joseph? After three days of anxiety, many of us would have asked, "Why have you done this *to me*?" or "Do you know how worried *I was*?" Mary, on the other hand, clearly refers to "us." This is a significant detail that reinforces Mary's strong charity. As we previously noted in the discussion of the Visitation, Mary was constantly concerned about the needs of others. Despite the fact that she was in the initial stages of her own pregnancy, Mary came to the aid of Elizabeth. Even though she was a guest at a wedding in Cana (John 2:1–11), she was concerned about the needs of the bride and groom. Mary's words, spoken during a time of great stress, reveal her caring nature. Aside from her own anxiety, she was concerned that her husband had to suffer. We can also see her charity displayed in the way she addressed Jesus. She didn't yell, she didn't threaten, she simply asked him why he stayed behind in Jerusalem.

Looking at Mary's question reminds us of a recurring theme throughout her life. She didn't have all the answers. Even though she was the Mother of the Savior, the Lord spoke to her through mystery. Mary certainly knew that Jesus was the Son of God. Even though the angel Gabriel informed her of this fact (Luke 1:35), however, she wasn't told all that his role would entail. That's precisely why she had to ask questions. She truly didn't understand why this happened. Did she and Joseph do something wrong? Were they neglecting their parental duties? Is this the way it's going to be for the Mother of God? What's next? Mary's question was in no way rhetorical. She sincerely wanted to know why Jesus stayed behind in Jerusalem, knowing that his absence would cause great anxiety.

What Mary was doing here is essentially what we do when we pray. Speaking to Jesus, the Blessed Mother asked about the meaning of his absence. She didn't fully understand the duties of being the Mother of God, and who can blame her? Being a parent is difficult enough, but Mary had the additional burden of her child also being her Savior. Where does she draw the line between demanding obedience from her Son and being obedient to her God? As was previously noted when Mary questioned the angel, she doesn't hesitate to ask questions in order to better understand God's will for her life. If she doesn't understand, how can she obey?

In addition to learning to imitate Mary's charity and desire to do God's will, there's another important lesson contained in this encounter. Sometimes God's answer is not the one we want to hear, especially when it involves suffering. Just like Mary, we often ask God many questions. Will you please heal my husband's illness? Can I please get this new job? Could you let my children return to church? Why are you letting me suffer? And, like the Blessed Mother, we often receive an unpleasant answer. Like it or not, crosses are part of our lives, and no one is exempt. Jesus and Mary both suffered greatly during their lifetimes. While God never promised to take away our problems entirely, he did promise he would not let us face our problems alone and to grant us his peace (Matthew 11:28). Mary understands this much better than we do. By asking questions, she sought to better understand God's will for her life.

When we are faced with difficulties and confusion, we would be wise to take a page out of her book. Instead of complaining or getting angry with the Lord, asking pertinent questions will set us on the road to doing his will. Instead of getting angry about our financial or medical problems, we can ask the Lord why he has us in this situation. We can also ask what he'd like us to learn from this experience. Likewise, we can request that he teach us how we can help others who may be experiencing the same problems. When we act in this manner, we imitate Mary. She knew the Lord would answer her questions and was willing to accept his answers. Give it a try in your own life, and don't be surprised when you experience tremendous peace.

The Message: Sometimes God speaks to us through mystery. By praying frequently, I can better understand his will for my life. Accepting God's answers will give us great peace.

Reflection Questions

1. When you are dealing with difficult problems in your life, do you ever ask God why? Rather than complain, do you ever ask him to show you how to make the best of the situation?

2. Have you ever lost your child, even momentarily? How did you feel? How do you think Mary and Joseph felt when they lost Jesus?

3. If you were in Mary's situation, what would you have said to Jesus upon finding him in the Temple? How do your words differ from Mary's?

4. Have you ever experienced a loss of Jesus in your life? How did it feel? What was your feeling when you rediscovered him? Are you separated from Christ now? How are you seeking to be reunited with him?

5. Recall the difficult situations you've experienced in your life. Does looking at them with hindsight reveal that some of them were blessings in disguise? What steps can you take to arrive at that realization as the problems are occurring, instead of after the fact?

CHAPTER 10
Anxiously Seeking Jesus

"Your father and I have been looking for you with great anxiety."
LUKE 2:48

A s the author of *A Worrier's Guide to the Bible: 50 Verses to Ease Anxieties*, I am well acquainted with the topic of anxiety. As I travel to different parishes to speak, I meet many people who are very worried. In some cases, I can't believe the serious problems these individuals are dealing with each day. When I give my talks about the topic of anxiety, the underlying theme is that God doesn't want us to worry. Looking through the pages of the Bible, we can find numerous instances where that message is proclaimed:

> "The LORD is my light and my salvation; whom should I fear? The LORD is my life's refuge; of whom should I be afraid?" (Psalm 27:1).
>
> "Do not let your hearts be troubled" (John 14:1).
>
> "I should like you to be free of anxieties" (1 Corinthians 7:32).

Although their worries may be different, those who are anxious all share a common bond. They know that worrying is painful and they want to eliminate it from their lives. Between medication, self-help books, and spiritual programs, people spend millions of dollars trying to rid themselves of anxiety. Therefore, one should be able to state with confidence that anxiety is always a bad thing, correct? Well, yes and no. When we refer to the anxiety that causes us to worry unceasingly, we can say it is not good for us and eliminating it is a worthwhile pursuit. There is another form of anxiety, however, that is actually a positive emotion and can be motivational in nature. In addition to being used negatively, the word "anxiety" can also be used in a positive sense. It can imply that one has a sense of urgency. For example, young children *anxiously* await the arrival of Christmas or their birthday. In this case, there is a sense of anticipation. They can't wait until the day arrives.

When Mary tells Jesus that she and Joseph were looking for him with "great anxiety," she was not implying they were sitting around worrying. Instead they were doing something productive: They were searching for him. Of course they were nervous. That's totally understandable given that their Son (who happens to be the Messiah) was missing. We look at this story with 2,000 years of hindsight that Mary and Joseph did not have. It's quite possible they assumed that due to their negligence, they could be affecting the salvation of future generations. As devout servants of God, they had every reason to feel anxious. But they didn't just sit around and worry. They did something about it. They searched and they searched and finally...they found Jesus.

In addition to Mary and Joseph's story, the Bible contains many other examples of individuals who anxiously pursued the Lord. Each Christmas season we're reminded of the shepherds who worked in the field "keeping...watch over their flock" (Luke 2:8). Visited by an angel, they were informed of the birth of Jesus, the Messiah. How did they react? Did they say, "Thanks for letting us know, but we have to get back to work?" Did they sit around and contemplate how this event would affect their lives? No. They were anxious to meet the Savior and so they dropped everything and traveled to Bethlehem...with great anxiety.

When the angels left them, the shepherds said to one another, "'Let us go, then, to Bethlehem to see this thing that has taken place, which the Lord has made known to us.' So they went in haste and found Mary and Joseph, and the infant lying in the manger" (Luke 2:15–16).

Bartimaeus was a blind beggar who was sitting by the roadside one day when something very special occurred. Jesus was leaving Jericho and passed by the beggar. When this poor blind man heard people talking about the presence of Jesus, he cried out, "Jesus, son of David, have pity on me" (Mark 10:47). Immediately, the people told him to be silent, but Bartimaeus was not fazed. Anxious to experience the healing touch of Christ, he cried out *all the more*, "Son of David, have pity on me" (Mark 10:48). At this point, Jesus called Bartimaeus over and restored his sight. Despite the crowd's attempt to stop him, the beggar's anxious pursuit of the Lord resulted in a powerful healing.

Need another example? Let's look at the familiar story of the storm at sea (Matthew 8:23–27). In a boat with his disciples, Jesus fell asleep. When a great storm arose, the disciples panicked and woke Jesus, crying, "Lord, save us! We are perishing!" (Matthew 8:25). It's hard to find a better example of someone searching anxiously for Jesus. The disciples were scared and desperate. Although we generally look at their behavior in a negative way (especially when we consider how Jesus criticized them for their lack of faith), they didn't just sit around and worry. They took action and sought the Lord. And, as we would expect, he calmed the sea and fixed the problem. Once again, we see a familiar pattern. Those who anxiously seek Jesus are rewarded.

Now let's examine our own lives. How important is it to us to be close to Jesus? Sadly, many people have little or no contact with him because "they're too busy." There's no doubt the world is a hectic place. It's very easy to lose touch with the Lord. We are constantly surrounded by noise, and it's sometimes hard to find quiet time for prayer. As a result, our relationship with Jesus suffers. What's sad is that we often don't care. As long as we're entertaining ourselves, we're happy, or at least we think we are. For years, my relationship with the Lord consisted of my presence at Mass once each week plus maybe a prayer or two when I was desperate. Outside of work and family, my free time was spent listening to the radio and watching TV for several hours each night. I had lots of excuses and reasons why I didn't have time to pray. Unfortunately, there was something missing in my life: a relationship with the Lord. What's even sadder is that I didn't realize it at the time. I just thought this was the way life was supposed to be. It wasn't until I finally began to make time for God that I understood how empty my life had become.

Aside from negligence, the other way we separate ourselves from the Lord is through sin. When we sin, we reject God and turn to an earthly pleasure. Although it's not usually a conscious rejection, it occurs by default whenever we commit a sin. Essentially sinning is turning away from God. Whether the sin is minor (venial) or major (mortal), there is some degree of separation that occurs between us and the Lord. Although we know the Lord is always anxious to welcome us back, some action is required on our part to repair the damage. In the case of mortal sin, the Church teaches that the only way to be reconciled with God is through the sacrament of reconciliation (also known as confession). With venial sin, an act of contrition or suitable act of repentance will suffice. But the point remains that, when we sin, we cause damage to our relationship with God and some action on our part is needed.

Whether it's due to sin or plain old carelessness, the fact of the matter is that we can become separated from Jesus. Just like Mary, Joseph, Bartimaeus, and the disciples in the boat, we can lose contact with him. These individuals all saw that something (or more accurately, "Someone") was missing in their lives, and they sought him out with great urgency. They were all able to find Jesus, but not without taking action. Is your relationship with the Lord in good shape? Do you need to get closer to him? If so, what are you doing to search for him "with great anxiety?"

Finally, there's one last important thing to consider about Mary's loss of Jesus. When we sin, we separate ourselves from the Lord. One of the downsides (if you can really call it a downside) of being conceived without original sin and never having committed a sin is that Mary didn't know what it was like to be separated from Jesus. Until this happened. In his infinite wisdom, the Lord knew there was only one way for Mary to feel what it's like to be distanced from him. After she went through this separation, she now understands what you and I feel when we sin. She isn't called the Refuge of Sinners for nothing. Our Lady is ready to welcome us back after we've gone astray. She will lead us to the loving arms of her Son so we can experience that same joyful reunion with Jesus that she and Joseph had in the Temple.

When we seek her assistance to get back in God's good graces, we can rest assured that she understands. Even though she was sinless, the loss of the Jesus in the Temple allows her to know how we feel when we lose the Lord through sin. Therefore, we should turn to her with confidence, knowing she knows exactly what we are going through. Throughout this book we'll see numerous examples of Mary's charity and how she put others before herself. She views our needs in the same way and won't desert us in our time of need.

The Message: When we become separated from Jesus due to sin or apathy, we should seek him with "great anxiety." If it's been a long time since you've received the sacrament of reconciliation, make a commitment to return.

Reflection Questions

1. How does it feel before you commit a sin? How about afterward? How anxious are you to seek forgiveness for your actions?

2. Discuss ways in which you could become closer to the Lord in your life.

3. Do you find it easy or difficult to confess your sins? How do you feel after you've done so? Discuss.

4. Think of people you know who have left the Catholic Church or who have lost their zeal for the faith. What steps can you take to help them return?

5. Recall situations in which you've felt separated from Jesus. How did it feel?

CHAPTER 11

Motherly Concern

"They have no wine."

JOHN 2:3

I always enjoy going to wedding receptions, especially when the food, music, and company are good. Looking back over the course of my life, I have lots of good memories spent celebrating the marriages of family and friends. Unfortunately we've all been to those affairs when one of the above ingredients isn't right. Those occasions are memorable as well, but for an entirely different reason. In the days of Jesus, wedding banquets were even more festive than they are today. The guests would drink, dance, and celebrate the union of the bride and groom. In some cases, especially if the families were wealthy, the celebration would last one or two weeks. Given the festive nature of these celebrations, it's easy to understand how running out of wine could really put a damper on the party. And that's exactly what happened one day in a Galilean village named Cana. As we read the account of this day (John 2:1–11), something unusual stands out: "On the third day there was a wedding in Cana in Galilee, and the mother of Jesus was there. Jesus and his disciples were also invited to the wedding" (John 2:1–2).

Doesn't it seem odd that Mary is the first guest listed by John? Even more unusual is that the presence of Jesus and his disciples is mentioned almost as an afterthought. If we take into consideration the fact that the author is known for his attention to detail, it becomes obvious that Mary is listed first for a reason. John obviously wanted to ensure that his readers take note of Mary's presence at the wedding. Why? Because she will play a prominent role in a very big event: the first miracle of Jesus.

Other than the guest list, the first real detail we get about the wedding is not a good one: The wine is gone! This was a big problem and certainly had the potential to kill the party, but something amazing was about to happen. Mary, once again illustrating her compassion and her watchfulness, informs her Son of the problem: "They have no wine" (John 2:3).

Before we look at Mary's words, let's reflect on a few details that could easily be missed. I don't know about you, but when I'm a guest at a wedding reception, my main objective is to enjoy myself. I think it's safe to say most of us feel the same way. The guests are there to have a good time and to celebrate. The staff, on the other hand, is there to ensure that the needs of the guests are met. Considering again John's propensity for details, who noticed the wine had run out? The headwaiter? The bride and groom? No, Mary (a guest) noticed the wine was gone. If someone else noticed it first, you can be sure the observant evangelist (many feel his attention to detail is because he was an eyewitness) would have pointed it out. Looking at our Lady's words, we can infer she's the one who noticed the problem. And what did she do? Did she run out and get more wine? Did she inform the staff? Did she threaten to leave unless the problem was corrected? No. She did something that should make us feel very good. She went straight to Jesus.

We can learn a lot about Mary by looking at how she handled the situation. Even though she was obviously concerned with the needs of others, she's humble enough to realize there's someone present who could better resolve the problem. Mary knew this issue should be handled by Jesus. Why should this make us feel good? Because looking at this situation reveals that Mary is so concerned with the needs of others that she often notices problems before they do (there is no indication the bride and groom or the headwaiter knew anything was wrong) and once she does, she brings the matter to her Son. In our lives we have many problems, some of which are very serious. While he was dying on the cross, Jesus appointed Mary as our spiritual Mother. Speaking to the "beloved disciple," the suffering Savior managed to utter the powerful words: "Behold, your mother" (John 19:27).

What does a mother do? She watches over her children and provides for their needs. Mary clearly exhibited these qualities at the wedding in Cana, and she is anxious to do the same for us. In addition to our known problems, Mary is also aware of unknown problems in our lives. Often spiritual in nature, these dangerous issues can adversely affect our lives as Christians and can even put our salvation in jeopardy. Sometimes without our knowledge, Mary intervenes and obtains graces that help us to overcome vices and bad habits. Have you ever been overcome with guilt about something you've done? Did that guilt lead you to change your ways or confess your sins? There's a good chance Mary had something to do with it. In addition to the unknown issues, she's always willing to lend a hand whenever we ask for her assistance with known problems.

Now, even if we believe Mary is watching out for us and is ready to deliver our needs to Jesus, the question remains as to how that will help us. After all, if Jesus isn't going to act on his Mother's request, her intercession won't do us much good. It's great she noticed there was no wine, but did the fact that she brought it to her Son's attention really matter? In order to assess the power of Mary's intercession, we need to fast-forward a few verses. After our Lady brought the problem to Jesus' attention (more on that later), he said something surprising: "Woman, how does your concern affect me? My hour has not yet come" (John 2:4).

Wow...what kind of response is this? Why did Jesus call his Mother, "Woman?" Sounds like he just put Mary in her place, doesn't it? In reality, he did nothing of the kind. In order to prove all is well with the Savior and his Mother, however, we need to look at some important details.

The first thing that needs to be looked at is what Jesus *didn't* say. Considering he's God and knows everything, do you really believe he didn't know the wine had run out? Of course he did. Therefore, notice he didn't criticize Mary for telling him something he already knew. Next we need to understand that people spoke differently 2,000 years ago and also that Jesus was most likely speaking in Aramaic, not English. Therefore, there are some cultural and translation issues that come into play here. Calling Mary by the title of "woman" could have been a sign of respect (a common practice in Jesus' time) or it could have been a reference to her role as the new Eve. In the Book of Genesis, Eve was referred to as "the woman." Mary is often called the new Eve because her obedience "undid" the damage done by the original Eve's disobedience. According to the Bible, there is another time when Jesus addressed his Mother as "woman." It happened at a time when it would be inconceivable that the Lord would disrespect his Mother: "When Jesus saw his mother and the disciple there whom he loved, he said to his mother, 'Woman, behold, your son'" (John 19:26).

Do you really think Jesus would choose this moment to insult Mary? Referring to his Mother as "woman" is in no way a sign of disrespect but rather a sign of great respect for her great faith and obedience.

What about the fact that our Lord said his hour had not yet come? Was he trying to tell his Mother to butt out? Hardly. He was simply stating a fact. As of the time he spoke these words, Jesus had not started his public ministry. His hour had not come, but that was about to change. After answering Mary, Jesus went on to perform his first miracle, thus officially inaugurating his public ministry. How effective was Mary's intercession for the bride and groom, who were about to be publicly humiliated at their wedding? Pretty effective, I'd say. Furthermore, do you remember what I said about Jesus knowing everything, including the fact that the wine had run out? Don't you think he could have just handled this matter on his own? And why did John (in his divinely inspired Gospel) want to call attention to Mary's presence at the wedding by listing her first? Could it be that Jesus wanted us to follow his example and turn to Mary with our problems, knowing she'd carry them to him? Sounds plausible to me.

Mary is a very special woman who has been used by God in remarkable ways. She wants to help us, and Jesus wants us to turn to her. Bring your problems to her today and you'll see amazing results. There are two recorded instances of Mary's intercession in the Bible. One occurred at the wedding in Cana and the other took place when she prayed with the Apostles in the upper room (Acts 1:14). The results? The first miracle of Jesus and the descent of the Holy Spirit on the Church on Pentecost. I'd say that's a pretty good track record, wouldn't you?

The Message: Jesus waited until Mary asked before performing his first miracle. By doing so, he gave us an example of her powerful intercession. Turn to her with confidence, knowing she'll take your requests directly to her Son.

Reflection Questions

1. Mary noticed there was no wine at the wedding feast. What is the "wine" that is missing in your own life? Have you asked for Mary's help?

2. If you were in Mary's position, how would you have handled the shortage of wine?

3. Does anything surprise you about Jesus' reaction to Mary's statement?

4. Why didn't Jesus just handle this situation by himself? Why did Mary have to be involved?

5. Recall some things that went wrong at your wedding reception or those you attended. How were they handled? Did the guests notice? Now, think of the wedding at Cana and what would have happened if Jesus had not produced more wine.

CHAPTER 12

Final Instructions

"Do whatever he tells you."

JOHN 2:5

S ometimes Catholics are accused of putting too much emphasis on Mary. Even devout Christians will sometimes tell us "she's not that important." One of the more popular reasons for this assertion is that there's very little mention of her in the Bible. As I've tried to illustrate throughout this book, the importance of Mary's message isn't dependent on the number of words spoken but rather on the quality of those words. Unfortunately we sometimes apply this logic to our prayer lives, thinking that more words makes for better prayer. Jesus discredited this assertion when he stated: "In praying, do not babble like the pagans, who think that they will be heard because of their many words" (Matthew 6:7).

Whether we're looking at prayer or ordinary conversation, speaking a lot of words doesn't necessarily make what you say important. Many of us express frustration when hearing a long speech by a politician who "said nothing." When analyzing the importance of someone's words, we should focus on the quality of the message and not the number of words used.

Rather than dwell on the fact that few of Mary's words are recorded in the Bible, I've tried to focus on the importance of those words. We now come to Mary's last recorded words in Scripture. These words were used to introduce the public ministry of Jesus. They were not only the last recorded words of Mary but the final recorded words before the beginning of the Lord's public ministry. Immediately after the Blessed Mother instructed the servants, Jesus took over and performed his first public miracle—changing the water into wine.

Before analyzing Mary's actual words, let's first take a broad look at the situation. Mary noticed that the wine had run out and informed her Son of the problem. He, in turn, replied that his hour had not come. Getting back to the argument that Jesus was "putting Mary in her place," wouldn't you have expected Mary to either respond with another plea or to ask why he was refusing her request? If she really cared about saving the day for the bride and groom (and she obviously did because she brought the matter to Jesus' attention), then doesn't it make sense that she would have asked her Son, "why not?" After all, as we've discovered from looking at her previous words, Mary wasn't afraid to ask questions. Instead, her response was to seek out the servers and tell them to follow the Lord's instructions. We can easily overlook the fact that, before this, the servers were not even mentioned. The encounter had been between Jesus and his Mother. Nobody else was involved. Why on earth would Mary, after supposedly being rebuked, go to the servers and tell them to get ready? The only realistic explanation is she expected Jesus to correct the problem. She understood his response and knew he was not putting her down. Mary knew that Jesus was about to act on her request. She understood that his "hour" was about to come.

The other important thing for us to note is that Mary knows when to get out of the way. She understands this is a job for the Lord and her work at the wedding is finished. Mary brought the problem to the attention of Jesus and trusted he would handle it. This is similar to John the Baptist's proclamation of "he must increase; I must decrease" (John 3:30). Mary and John both understood that their role was to call attention to Jesus and not to steal the show. That illustrates profound humility and is worthy of imitation. How many times in our lives do we try to control situations that would be best handled by the Lord? While God expects us to take action and try solutions, there often comes a point when we have to let go and trust in his providence. Knowing how to recognize that point can be difficult and requires a great deal of humility and trust. Looking at the example of people like Mary and John the Baptist can help us to remember that sometimes we just have to get out of the way and let God do his thing.

Now let's look at Mary's words. In five simple words, our Lady tells us all we need to know about getting to heaven. Her words are so powerful and so complete that any future words would have been superfluous. God understood that and, as a result, these were Mary's last recorded words in the Bible. By telling the servers to do whatever Jesus commands, she gives them a solution to the immediate problem. And by including these words in the inspired text, the Lord gives each of us a guidebook for getting to heaven.

Looking at this episode from a historical perspective, Mary told the servers to obey the commands of her Son. Obviously, they listened to her. In fact, they were so intent on doing what Jesus said that when he commanded them to fill the jars with water, John tells us they filled them "to the brim" (John 2:7). They weren't messing around. No filling the jars halfway...they filled them right to the top. Then they awaited the next instruction from the Lord. Jesus instructed them to draw out some of the liquid and take it to the headwaiter. They obeyed. I don't know about you, but I'd be a little hesitant. At this point, there is no indication there is anything in these jars except water. If I were to bring water to the headwaiter, I'd run the risk of looking foolish. But they didn't seem to care, choosing to listen to Mary's advice and follow the instructions of Jesus. After tasting the liquid, the headwaiter called over the bridegroom and complimented him on the excellent quality of this wine. Jesus had performed his first miracle and transformed water into wine. As a result, his disciples "began to believe in him" (John 2:11). The public ministry of Jesus had begun.

Continuing with a historical look at this miracle, let's recap the key points. Mary alerted Jesus that the wine had run out. After listening to his response, she instructed the servers to listen to the Lord's instructions. They obeyed and proceeded to fill the jars with water. Upon being told to bring some of the "water" to the headwaiter, they did so. The headwaiter tasted the "water" (which was now wine) and praised the bridegroom for saving the best wine for last. All of this came about after the servers obeyed Jesus at Mary's request. If they hadn't listened to him, who knows what might have happened? Could Jesus have performed the miracle without waiting for Mary's request? Absolutely, but he chose not to. He waited until she notified him of the problem.

The lesson of this miracle can (and should) be applied to our own lives. We all have a shortage of something in our lives. It could be spiritual (faith, charity, patience) or it could be temporal (money, friends, health). Ultimately, however, the biggest "need" in our lives is the need for the grace that will help us get to heaven. As the wedding at Cana illustrates, Mary is watching over us and already knows about the problems and needs in our lives. When you bring the issues to her attention, however, you express your love and trust in her...and that's good. By looking at the biblical account of what took place at Cana, we can infer that she will take our needs directly to Jesus and will not try to fix them by herself. Once she does that, however, our work is not finished. She then asks us to do something very important. Mary instructs us to do whatever Jesus tells us. While that may sound vague and could be misconstrued as giving us a lot of wiggle room, it's actually a very strong and specific request by our Lady. Jesus founded a Church (Matthew 16:18–19) and gave his Church the right to teach authoritatively. And Mary always points us to Jesus, that is: Do whatever our Lord tells us. Today we have the benefit of 2,000 years of Church history to help us understand these words in context, as the Catholic Church continues to hold them sacred and relay them to us.

In our society, the problem of relativism is pervasive, even among Catholics. The idea that one can pick and choose which Church teachings to obey is becoming increasing popular. Still wanting to hold on to their Catholic identity, many people are rejecting the more challenging teachings of the Church while claiming to embrace Catholicism. This idea not only goes against the wishes of Mary, as expressed in her instructions to "do whatever he tells you" at Cana, but it is in opposition to Jesus' final instructions to his Apostles. As he sent them forth to "make disciples of all nations," the Lord instructed them to teach "all that I have commanded you" (Matthew 28:19–20). Mary not only understood the necessity of obeying the Lord's commands, she lived them. Her entire life was spent doing God's will. For this reason, it's extremely fitting that God chose these words to be her final words in the Bible. When she first spoke these words to the servers 2,000 years ago, it proved to be good advice. They obeyed, and the water was changed into wine. Her message is also directed to each of us. Like the servers, we can choose to obey her instruction. While it's not a wise choice, we can also use our free will and disregard her directions. If we choose that option, however, chances are good that our Judgment Day won't go as smoothly as if we had listened.

The Message: Jesus said, "If you love me, you will keep my commandments" (John 14:15). Sadly, we sometimes ignore his words and disobey the teachings of the Catholic Church. Mary understood the importance of obedience and urges us to always do what her Son commands. By doing so, we'll be assured of reaching eternal life in heaven.

Reflection Questions

1. Put yourselves in the place of the servers. What do you think was going through their minds when Jesus asked them to fill the jars with water? How about when he told them to take some of the beverage to the headwaiter?

2. In your opinion, how would Mary have reacted if she didn't believe that Jesus would produce the wine?

3. There is no indication that the bride and groom ever knew there was a problem. Has something similar ever happened in your life? How did you feel once you found out the problem was corrected? Relieved? Grateful?

4. What Church teachings are the most difficult for you? Do you attempt to discern why the Church teaches as she does?

5. What do you think would have happened if the servers had not obeyed Mary's instructions? Who would have been impacted the most by their refusal to listen?

PART II

Unspoken Words

CHAPTER 13

Pondering in Her Heart

"But she was greatly troubled at what was said and
pondered what sort of greeting this might be."

Luke 1:29

"And Mary kept all these things, reflecting on them in her heart."

Luke 2:19

"He went down with them and came to Nazareth, and
was obedient to them; and his mother kept all these
things in her heart."

Luke 2:51

Most of us are very busy. Unfortunately we're sometimes so busy with unimportant things that we
miss out on things that really matter. For instance,
do you make it a point to listen to God each day? Do you ask
him how you can best serve him in your daily activities? If your
answer is "no" or "not really," you are not alone. In fact, most
of us are so busy running around that we don't take the time to
listen to God. The biblical account of Martha and Mary (Luke
10:38–42) illustrates that very situation. Our Lord went to the
town of Bethany to visit his friends, Martha and Mary, and was
met with two very different reactions. When he arrived, Martha
waited on the Lord hand and foot. She wanted to ensure that
he was treated with a great amount of hospitality. As Martha

slaved to serve Jesus, however, her sister Mary "sat beside the Lord at his feet listening to him speak" (Luke 10:39). Overcome by frustration (and probably exhaustion), Martha attempted to get Jesus to persuade Mary to join in the serving. Siding with Mary, Jesus gave a surprising reply: "Martha, Martha, you are anxious and worried about many things. There is need of only one thing. Mary has chosen the better part and it will not be taken from her" (Luke 10:41–42).

While not saying that Martha is wrong (work is a necessary and noble endeavor), Jesus pointed out the necessity for spiritual contemplation. Martha was so busy serving that she had become anxious and worried. If she paused for a minute and took some time to listen to Jesus (like Mary), there's a good chance she would have heard him warn about the uselessness of anxiety. Martha had her Lord and Savior in her house and was so busy that she didn't take the time to listen to him speak. How many times do we do the same thing? God speaks to us in many different ways, but we often fail to listen.

Even though we may attend Mass on Sunday, we are often preoccupied. Our distraction can cause us to daydream through the Scripture readings. As a result, we miss out on God's message for us. Sadly, missing his message could also mean we fail to hear God communicate his will to us. The Lord has a specific plan for each of our lives, and one of the ways he delivers the details of that plan is through the pages of the Bible. Simply being present at Mass doesn't guarantee we will hear his message. We have to *listen*. Whether we are hearing the Bible proclaimed at Mass or reading it at home, we make a mistake when we treat God's written word as just another book. The Bible contains a series of personal messages from God to each of us. In order to hear that message, however, some effort on our part is required.

Another way God speaks to us is through prayer. Whether we use formal prayers, such as the Our Father or Hail Mary, or simply use our own words, prayer is a conversation with God. Sometimes we speak and sometimes he speaks. Due to the fact that we live in a world that is filled with noise, however, we sometimes find it difficult to hear God's voice. Listening for God's voice can be difficult and requires some practice. While we'd prefer that he'd speak in a loud, booming voice that is unmistakable, that's not usually the way the Lord interacts with us. The prophet Elijah learned this lesson when he tried to hear God speak to him at Mount Horeb (1 Kings 19:9–18). Expecting the Lord to speak in a powerful way, the prophet encountered strong winds, an earthquake, and a fire, none of which contained God's message. It wasn't until Elijah heard a "still small voice" that he knew the Lord was speaking to him. If he hadn't been paying careful attention, the prophet could have easily missed God's instructions to anoint Elisha as his successor.

In the same way, we often miss the Lord's message because we simply don't hear his voice. When I pray, I have a tendency to speak *a lot*. If I'm not careful, I can easily get carried away and never give the Lord a chance to do some of the talking. Prayer should always be a dialogue and not a monologue. If we truly want to follow God's will in our lives, we have to give him a chance to tell us what he wants us to do. Do you remember how the Lord first called the prophet Samuel? While ministering to the Lord under Eli, a priest, young Samuel kept hearing a voice calling him while he tried to sleep (1 Samuel 3:1–18). Several times Samuel heard the voice and went to Eli who said, "I did not call you." Finally, after realizing that it was the Lord who was calling the young boy, Eli provided some excellent advice: "Go to sleep, and if you are called, reply, 'Speak, LORD, for your servant is listening'" (1 Samuel 3:9).

Samuel obeyed and, as a result, the Lord was able to give him a mission. If we want to serve God and do his will, we need to make these words our own. The Lord will not usually force his message upon us. Instead, he'll wait until we ask and listen.

Mary understood this and provides us a great example of how to listen to God's voice and discern his message. Surprisingly, she wasn't given all the answers up front. Just like us, the Blessed Mother had to prayerfully discern God's will for her life. In Luke's Gospel, we're told she "pondered, reflected and kept things in her heart." These are the characteristics of someone who definitely made the time to converse with the Lord. If we could learn to follow Mary's example, there's no telling how much good we could do. Looking at it logically, wouldn't it be a lot easier to do God's will if we knew what he wanted us to do? That information is only going to be obtained if we take the time to listen and meditate, in order to prepare our hearts for God's mission or call to us.

People often ask me how I knew God was calling me to be a full-time Catholic evangelist. It took several years of intense prayer, spiritual direction, and a job layoff before I was sure. While the experience was frustrating for me, I noticed a great benefit from my process of discernment. Because I was praying so much, I grew a lot closer to the Lord. Even though it seemed like I was just "bending his ear," I wasn't. In reality, I was learning to depend on him and converse with him frequently. As human beings, we sometimes fail to see the big picture. Using our limited perspective, we have a tendency to question the Lord's providential plan for our lives. We can't understand how anything good can come out of financial struggles or sickness. And we question why God would let us suffer. Rather than complain and pull away from him, however, the best solution is to meditate and discern our next step. Sometimes that will involve taking action, and other times it will simply require us to endure unpleasant circumstances that unfold in our lives. How do we know which course of action we should take? We will know by imitating the Blessed Mother and learning to converse with God frequently.

Mary's actions (pondering, reflecting, and keeping things in her heart) don't seem to indicate that God's message was immediately apparent to her. It was something that had to be worked at and processed over a period of time. By imitating Mary's example of "pondering and reflecting" on the events in my life, my relationship with the Lord strengthened and I was better able to understand what he wanted me to do. If you find yourself in a similar situation, I urge you to do the same thing. If the Lord revealed his plans to Mary in mystery, he's likely to do the same thing with us. If you hear the booming voice or see a divine thunderbolt, good for you. But if you're like Mary (and me), continue to ponder and reflect, knowing you're in good company.

The Message: Determining God's will often requires us to meditate on the events in our lives. Just as Mary pondered on things happening to her, so must we. It may take some time, but doing so will enable us to discover his plan for our lives.

Reflection Questions

1. Are you surprised that Mary needed to meditate frequently? What possible benefits could have resulted from her having to do this?

2. How can you apply Mary's practice to the mysteries in your life?

3. How does God speak to you? Is there a particular place that best enables you to hear him?

4. When you pray, do you spend more time speaking or listening?

5. We know that God speaks through the Bible. Name some other ways in which the Lord speaks to the world today?

CHAPTER 14

Love of Neighbor

"During those days Mary set out and traveled to the
hill country in haste to a town of Judah, where she
entered the house of Zechariah and greeted Elizabeth."

LUKE 1:39–40

One of the more challenging aspects of being a Christian is loving our neighbor...always. Sure, it's no problem loving those who love us back and who are lovable. When it comes to displaying charity to those who hate us or those who we find to be annoying, however, we often conveniently overlook this important command. Our desire to love our neighbor also decreases when it becomes too much trouble. How many times do I put off helping someone because "I have my own problems?" While doing this is a common practice, it's one that should be addressed and discontinued. Why?

Jesus tells us, "This is my commandment: love one another as I love you" (John 15:12).

"If anyone says, 'I love God,' but hates his brother, he is a liar; for whoever does not love a brother whom he has seen cannot love God whom he has not seen. This is the commandment we have from him: whoever loves God must also love his brother" (1 John 4:20–21).

If looking at the words of Jesus and John make you a bit uncomfortable, join the club. Not only are they challenging, but they can be downright frightening. When we consider we're all going to be judged one day, these words can become motivational. Reading these commands should spur us on to greater love of our neighbor. But rather than dwell on the negative, let's look at the positive aspect of loving one another. There are some great benefits to loving others, even when we may not feel like it. For one thing, when we love one another, we express our love for the Lord. When discussing the final judgment, Jesus speaks of rewarding those who provided him with food, drink, and clothing. He then proceeds to address an obvious question:

> "Then the righteous will answer him and say, 'Lord, when did we see you hungry and feed you, or thirsty and give you drink? When did we see you a stranger and welcome you, or naked and clothe you? When did we see you ill or in prison, and visit you?' And the king will say to them in reply, 'Amen, I say to you, whatever you did for one of these least brothers of mine, you did for me'" (Matthew 25:37–40).

When we serve our neighbor (our friend, our enemy, the annoying coworker), we serve God. Many times when I'm giving a talk at a parish, I mention that it's easy for us to love the Lord when we're sitting in church with our prayer book. There is generally a feeling of peace that comes over us when we're in God's house. Our problems fade away, there's a calm stillness in the air, and all is well. When it's time to venture outside the church doors and into the "real world," things change. All of a sudden, we're forced to deal with deadlines, traffic, financial issues, and...annoying people. Sometimes we don't even make it out of the church parking lot before people are getting on our nerves. That same person with whom we shared the sign of peace just pulled out in front of our car and we're livid. We might even mutter (or loudly proclaim) our feelings about him or his driving abilities. By the time we get home, we're overwhelmed by all of the important things we have to do. Throughout the course of the workweek, we find ourselves being increasingly consumed by deadlines and frustrated by those individuals who drive us crazy. As we fight our way through the week, that feeling of peace we experienced on Sunday seems like a distant memory. What happened? Unfortunately, we lost sight of what true charity means. Not only do we need to practice it in church but out in the world as well.

Mary understood what it meant to love her neighbor. She knew that, just like Jesus, her main purpose was to serve others and not to be served (Matthew 20:28). That desire to serve others can be seen in her visit to Elizabeth (Luke 1:39–56). After informing Mary she had been chosen to become the Mother of the Savior and that her pregnancy would come about through the power of the Holy Spirit, the angel told her that Elizabeth (her elderly relative) was six months pregnant. Putting aside the issues in her own life (and there were many: how to tell her family, the impact to her wedding with Joseph, that her Son will be the Messiah, etc.), Mary began the arduous journey to visit her relative. Although we're not told the exact location of Elizabeth's home, a journey from Nazareth to the hill country would take several days. Not only does this prove that Mary put the needs of others ahead of her own needs, but Luke provides us with some details that show just *how much* she cared. We're told that Mary left "in haste." In other words, she didn't waste any time feeling sorry for herself or worrying about the problems in her own life. Someone needed her, and not only did she respond, but she responded in a hurry.

When Mary arrived at the home of Elizabeth, she was not alone. She brought Jesus with her. As a result, Elizabeth was able to experience the Real Presence of her Lord and Savior. This was a great blessing and resulted in both Elizabeth and her son (John the Baptist) being touched by the Lord's presence. In his encyclical "*Ecclesia de Eucharistia*," Blessed Pope John Paul II referred to Mary as the "first tabernacle." As a result, Elizabeth was able to worship the still invisible Jesus, present in Mary's body. Although we often fail to recognize it, we all have the capability to fulfill the same role. When we receive Jesus in Holy Communion, we also become human tabernacles. When we exit the church into that world filled with so many challenges and people that drive us crazy, we bring Jesus with us. What do we do with him? Like Mary, do we bring him to those people in our daily lives? Do we travel "in haste" to help them? Or, after receiving the Body, Blood, soul, and divinity of Jesus, do we leave him behind and tend to our own affairs?

There are many people in the world around us who do not know Jesus. They may have heard of him, but they don't know him. Some of these individuals are the people in our life: family, friends, coworkers, fellow shoppers in the grocery store, etc. We can make a huge difference in their lives by allowing them to meet the Lord. This is precisely what Mary did for Elizabeth. On the other hand, we can keep Jesus to ourselves or, worse yet, ignore him and leave him in the pew when we exit the church. The choice is ours. Mary should be our role model when it comes to charity. She ignored her own pressing needs, choosing to serve Elizabeth, and as a result, she had a tremendous impact on someone's life. Don't write off the impact you can have on the lives of those around you. They need Jesus in their lives. He wants to be shared with others, as Mary understood well.

Follow her lead and ask for her intercession. The world can be a very dark place, but by bringing Jesus (the light of the world) to those around you, you can turn their darkness to light.

The Message: What are we doing to bring Jesus to those around us? Mary put aside her own needs and reached out to Elizabeth, who was then greatly blessed by an encounter with Jesus. We should look for ways to bring the Lord into the lives of those around us, including those people who we find to be difficult.

Reflection Questions

1. Name some ways in which you can bring Jesus to those in your life.

2. Think of a person in your life you find to be annoying. How can you show this individual the Lord's love?

3. What do you think was going on in Mary's head as she journeyed to the home of Elizabeth? She obviously was able to cast aside her own needs and reach out to her relative. Are there issues in your life that are preventing you from reaching out to others?

4. Do you find it easy or difficult to love your enemies? Do you pray for the ability to forgive as Jesus did?

5. Who is the most difficult person in your life? Say a brief prayer for that person.

CHAPTER 15

A Powerful Endorsement

"While he was speaking, a woman from the crowd
called out and said to him, 'Blessed is the womb that
carried you and the breasts at which you nursed.'
He replied, 'Rather, blessed are those who hear the
word of God and observe it.'"

LUKE 11:27–28

In every Bible verse included in this book, Mary is either saying or doing something, except for this one. In fact, Luke gives no indication as to whether the Mother of Jesus is even present during this encounter between Jesus and a crowd of people. It seems an unlikely verse to be part of a book on Mary's words in Scripture, doesn't it? Furthermore, it appears that Jesus is putting down his Mother when this unidentified woman spoke out on her behalf. Why would I include a statement that makes Mary look bad? Wouldn't it kill the effectiveness of my message? In reality, this may be one of the most powerful verses in the book. For nowhere else in the Bible does Jesus so boldly praise his Mother and hold her up as a model for all Christians.

Before delving into the particulars of this encounter, let's lay some groundwork. Anyone who's ever tried to get a new job understands the value of a good reference. As the old saying goes, "It's not *what* you know, it's *who* you know." Having someone vouch for your skills can be invaluable when it comes to getting the nod from a potential employer. Even more important is delivering a reference from someone who is prestigious or greatly respected. A person applying for a marketing position who has a reference from Donald Trump is going to be taken much more seriously than if that recommendation comes from a young coworker with two years of experience.

The power of a good endorsement can be found in the pages of the Bible. As he prepared to begin his public ministry, Jesus allowed himself to be baptized by John the Baptist in the Jordan River (Mark 1:9). Anyone who witnessed this event saw something very special take place on that day. Although it wasn't necessary, Jesus received a powerful endorsement. It's so strong that I find it hard to believe that anyone who heard it wouldn't take Christ's mission very seriously. After Jesus came out of the water, the heavens opened, and the Holy Spirit descended upon him. Then a voice came from heaven: "You are my beloved Son; with you I am well pleased" (Mark 1:11).

Throughout this book, I've pointed to Mary's appearances in the Bible and offered reasons why you should admire and respect her. While I hope you arrive at this conclusion after reading my words, it couldn't hurt if someone with *a lot* more authority than me made the same point. Just as God the Father gave his stamp of approval to Jesus on the day of his baptism, Mary will also get a divine recommendation. And just like the aforementioned one, it will be documented in the pages of the Bible.

Now let's set the scene. Jesus has just driven out a demon, and the crowds were amazed (Luke 11:27). A woman in the crowd began to sing the praises of Mary. Obviously this woman was very excited, as Luke indicates that she called out while Jesus was still speaking. She declared blessed the "womb that carried him" and the "breasts at which he nursed." These praises are reminiscent of Elizabeth's praise of Mary: "Most blessed are you among women, and blessed is the fruit of your womb" (Luke 1:42).

Certainly Mary is blessed to be the Mother of God. Our Lady acknowledged that when she stated "all generations will call me blessed" (Luke 1:48). While the woman in the crowd wasn't saying anything untrue, Jesus felt the need to amplify her statement. The Lord agreed with the woman that Mary was indeed blessed. In fact, he began his reply by proclaiming the same thing. Jesus, however, wanted to take it a step further. The woman called Mary blessed because she was Jesus' biological Mother. While not disputing her statement, however, the Lord pointed out that his Mother is blessed to a greater degree because of her desire to always hear and observe the word of God.

As we examine our Lady's life in the pages of the Bible, it's easy to document her desire to follow God's will. Our first glimpse of Mary featured her being visited by the angel Gabriel. During this visit, she was informed that she had been chosen to become the Mother of the Savior, Jesus Christ. After making sure she understood the details, Mary gave her assent. In the next chapter we'll see how she stood by as her Son was crucified. Throughout her life, Mary accepted and followed the will of God, even when it involved the discomfort of suffering. That is why Jesus was able to affirm Mary's faithfulness to the will of God.

Did you notice exactly what Jesus said about Mary when he was praising her? Although you probably get the general idea, there's a subtle point that deserves to be highlighted. The Lord declared that Mary is blessed because she heard and observed the word of God. As you and I know, it's totally possible to hear the word of God and not observe it. This idea is explored in the parable of the Sower (Matthew 13:1–9). In this familiar story, Jesus told of a sower who planted seeds in different places.

Some of the seeds fell along the path, some fell on rocky ground or among thorns, and some fell on good soil. Where the seed landed determined how much grain was produced. In order to ensure they understood, Jesus explained the meaning of the parable to his disciples. In Scripture, Jesus magnifies what it is to hear the word of God:

> "The seed sown on the path is the one who hears the word of the kingdom without understanding it, and the evil one comes and steals away what was sown in his heart. The seed sown on rocky ground is the one who hears the word and receives it at once with joy. But he has no root and lasts only for a time. When some tribulation or persecution comes because of the word, he immediately falls away. The seed sown among thorns is the one who hears the word, but then worldly anxiety and the lure of riches choke the word and it bears no fruit" (Matthew 13:19–22).

Mary not only heard the word of God, but she observed it. She was the "fertile soil" that welcomed the "seed," causing it to grow and bear great fruit (Matthew 13:23). This is the point Jesus was trying to make when he praised his Mother. She always sought to hear the word of God (which often involved prayer and meditation, as we've discussed) and, more importantly, she put that word in practice. Mary lived the word of God.

How many times do you and I fail at this? Despite our good intentions, we fail to hear and observe the word of God. Distracted by our many problems and concerns, we'll often sit at Mass and ignore God's word as it is proclaimed to us. And, if we do hear the readings, how often do we apply them to our daily lives? If you're like me, you probably do this a lot less than you should.

Rather than be discouraged, however, we should focus on Jesus' endorsement of Mary. The Lord tells us that his Mother knew how to put this difficult concept into practice. Jesus' words to the woman in the crowd are his only recorded words of praise for Mary, but don't let it confuse you. In that one sentence, Jesus affirmed his Mother in the greatest way possible. As we struggle to hear and observe God's word, we should turn to Mary. Her intercession can help us to hear God's word more clearly and then follow Jesus. With her help, we can look forward to hearing Jesus say the following about us on our Judgment Day: *"Blessed are those who hear the word of God and observe it."*

The Message: Jesus praised Mary for her desire to hear and observe the word of God. We should strive to do the same thing.

Reflection Questions

1. Do you strive to hear God speak on a daily basis? What obstacles do you encounter? Identify some ways to overcome those obstacles.

2. After witnessing Jesus drive out the demon, why do you think the woman in the crowd was inspired to praise Mary? What do you think she was trying to say?

3. Look at the various references to Mary in the Bible and find evidence of her listening to and obeying the word of God.

4. Do you find it difficult to put God's word into practice? If so, why?

5. How do you handle failure when it comes to putting God's word into practice? Do you sometimes fall into despair? Do you receive the sacrament of penance? How about asking God for the grace to do better?

CHAPTER 16

Faithful to the End

"Standing by the cross of Jesus were his mother
and his mother's sister, Mary the wife of Clopas,
and Mary of Magdala."

JOHN 19:25

There's nothing like a loyal friend. Knowing that someone will be there for you no matter what can be very comforting. If we think about it, most of us can come up with a list of people we know we can always count on. On the other hand, we can also compose a list of those individuals who weren't there when we needed them. Unfortunately, there's a good chance the second list will be longer than the first one. Loyalty is a great quality, but sometimes it's difficult to practice. Many people have good intentions but lose heart once they encounter difficulties.

One of my favorite examples of loyalty comes from the Old Testament. In the Book of Ruth, we are introduced to Naomi, a woman who journeyed with her husband and two sons from Bethlehem to Moab in order to obtain relief from a famine. Eventually Naomi's husband died and her two sons married Moabite women, Orpah and Ruth. When the husbands of Orpah and Ruth died, Naomi told them she was returning to Bethlehem. As they set out together, Naomi encouraged the women to stay in Moab and return to the homes of their families. Reluctantly, Orpah agreed. Ruth, on the other hand, spoke some of the most eloquent words in Scripture and vowed to remain with her mother-in-law:

Ruth said, "Do not press me to go back and abandon you! Wherever you go I will go, wherever you lodge I will lodge. Your people shall be my people and your God, my God. Where you die I will die, and there be buried. May the LORD do thus to me, and more, if even death separates me from you!" (Ruth 1:16–17).

Motivated by love, Ruth refused to abandon her mother-in-law, even when encouraged to do so. As a result, she left her homeland of Moab and all of its security in order to remain with Naomi. I'm sure this was difficult for Ruth. When her husband died, it would have been much easier for her to return to the familiar house of her mother, who would have provided security at a time when she most needed it. Instead, Ruth chose to journey to Bethlehem with Naomi. Motivated by her love for her mother-in-law, Ruth acted in a way that was very uncommon in her era and would have required a great deal of courage. Looking beyond her own needs, she sought to comfort Naomi. Even though it would involve a certain degree of suffering, Ruth accepted it and believed that a greater good would come.

When I was in college, I decided I wanted to put some bulk on my skinny body, so I decided to start working out with weights. My plan was to do this every other day. I was very motivated in the beginning, sometimes wishing I could do it every day. As the weeks progressed, my desire began to decrease. Eventually I gave it up because it became too much work. After I graduated from college, I once again thought about weight training. Thinking that maybe I lost interest because I was exercising in my parents' basement, I decided to join a gym. Being around other like-minded people and having to pay a membership fee will definitely motivate me to persist, I reasoned. After a few months of full-speed-ahead workouts, I skipped a day because I was too tired to go to the gym. That one missed day turned into two...and three. I never went back. Despite my best intentions, I quit once again. Just like before, the suffering got the best of me, and I took the easy way out.

Although my repeated failures at the gym were frustrating, they didn't have a major impact on my life. In addition, this experience taught me something about myself. If things get too difficult for me, I have a tendency to give up. While coming to this realization was not the most pleasant discovery, it did serve as an eye-opener. It made me aware of a potential problem in my life. As a result of discovering this weakness in my personality, I've learned to compensate for it and persevere through many difficult situations. And while it can still be a struggle, I have learned to deal with my weakness and achieve positive results. One of the most important applications of this technique has involved putting it into practice with my faith.

We can give up or fail at many things in life and still experience no long-term repercussions. As was the case with my weightlifting sessions, I was able to learn something from my lack of success and move on. No real harm done. We've all quit doing something because it got too burdensome. There are some things in life, however, that we do not want to quit even if they involve lots of hard work or suffering. The most important of these "never quit" things is our relationship with Jesus. No matter how frustrated we become with events in our lives or how little joy we're feeling, giving up on our relationship with the Lord is *always* a bad idea!

God loves us so much that no matter what we do, he'll never desert us (Joshua 1:5). That's a very comforting thought and should make us all feel very good. On the other hand, we can (and often do) walk away from him. Whenever we sin, that's exactly what takes place. Jesus became man so he could die for *our* sins. In reality, you and I should have been hanging on the cross instead of him. Because we were incapable of repairing the rift between God and man, however, Jesus took our place. More importantly, he did it willingly because of his great love for us. He also grants us the great privilege of sharing in his suffering and helping him with the mission of redemption. As St. Paul states: "Now I rejoice in my sufferings for your sake, and in my flesh I am filling up what is lacking in the afflictions of Christ on behalf of his body, which is the church" (Colossians 1:24).

As members of the mystical body of Christ (the Church), we are invited to willingly unite our suffering with the Lord's. Although nothing was lacking in his sacrifice, what is sometimes lacking is our participation. We often reject our crosses and sometimes turn away from the Lord completely when the going gets tough. Although the choice is ours to make, is that really the best way to express our gratitude for all he's done for us?

Mary never deserted Jesus. Unlike most of the Apostles, she was present at his crucifixion. Not only was she there, but she stood by the cross. As a parent, I can't imagine anything more painful than watching my child suffer. Despite all of the torment that it involved, Mary was there. She could have passed, explaining that it would be too painful. There's a good chance that many of us would have chosen that option. Mary, on the other hand, knew she had to be there. By uniting her suffering with the Lord's, she was doing what we're all called to do—endure suffering out of love for our Lord and others.

Suffering is part of life. Unfortunately, we often waste it by running away from it. Jesus embraced his cross, as did Mary. Each day we are given the choice to complain about our problems or accept them. We can curse our bad luck or accept it as being

God's will. Still, we are never asked to make our way forward by ourselves. The Lord will send us the grace we need to endure even the heaviest of crosses. While he never promised to take all of our burdens away, he does promise to lighten our load and grant us his peace. Mary can and will assist us if we ask for her help. She knows that suffering can be a challenge, but she also knows that remaining close to Jesus is the only way to go through life.

The Message: How many times do we desert Jesus by rejecting the suffering that comes into our lives? Mary suffered with him on Calvary, and we're invited to do the same. Are we willing?

Reflection Questions

1. Think about the fact that Jesus loves you so much that he was willing to suffer and die for your sins. Do you feel the desire to express your gratitude? How?

2. Put yourself in Mary's place as she watched her Son be tortured and murdered. What would be going through your mind if you were the Lord's parent? How would you react?

3. Call to mind the various crosses in your life. Are you rejecting any of them? How could you better embrace them?

4. Recall instances of suffering that you've encountered in your life. Looking back, identify some positives that resulted from enduring these trials.

5. Identify people in your life who are suffering in some way. Make a decision to help them. Whether it's by praying, fasting, or offering words of encouragement, your actions can bring them comfort.

CHAPTER 17

The Last Image

"All these devoted themselves with one accord to prayer, together with some women, and Mary the mother of Jesus, and his brothers."

ACTS 1:14

How important is prayer? Moses prayed for his people after they had sinned (Numbers 21:7), Job prayed for his friends (Job 42:10), and St. Paul instructs us to "pray without ceasing" (1 Thessalonians 5:17). The Bible tells us Jesus prayed several times, most notably on the night before he died. Therefore it's only fitting that Mary's last appearance in Scripture finds her praying with the Apostles. Given the fact that she had a propensity for meditation, this shouldn't come as a surprise. The Bible tells us that, throughout her life, Mary pondered and kept things in her heart. What a perfect way to remember our Lady—as a *woman of prayer.*

One of the biggest mistakes we can make is to underestimate the value of prayer. Unfortunately it's something we do all of the time. It happens when we lose sight of God's power and focus solely on earthly things. Living and functioning in the world can easily cause us to deny that the Lord can still perform miracles. Often those miracles will only come about when we pray. While there are some gifts God gives to us whether or not we ask for them, others require our prayers before they are granted. For instance, most people who experience a conversion

103

do so without having asked for it. Something happens, and they hear and respond to God's call. This is what happened with the Apostles. They were performing their ordinary duties and were called by the Lord. They didn't have to specifically pray that they would be chosen. On the other hand, many of the healings Jesus performed came about because the individuals asked, as can be seen in the following Scripture passages:

"Soon a woman whose daughter had an unclean spirit heard about him. She came and fell at his feet. The woman was a Greek, a Syrophoenician by birth, and she begged him to drive the demon out of her daughter" (Mark 7:25–26).

"Now there was a man full of leprosy in one of the towns where he was; and when he saw Jesus, he fell prostrate, pleaded with him, and said, 'Lord, if you wish, you can make me clean'" (Luke 5:12).

"Then he returned to Cana in Galilee, where he had made the water wine. Now there was a royal official whose son was ill in Capernaum. When he heard that Jesus had arrived in Galilee from Judea, he went to him and asked him to come down and heal his son, who was near death" (John 4:46–47).

In each of these cases, people approached Jesus and asked for healings—they prayed. As a result, their requests were granted. Would the healings have occurred if they hadn't asked? Maybe, maybe not. What we do know is that, in each of these cases, Jesus responded to a request for healing by granting the request. This makes perfect sense given the fact that he stated:

"Ask and it will be given to you; seek and you will find; knock and the door will be opened to you. For everyone who asks, receives; and the one who seeks, finds; and to the one who knocks, the door will be opened" (Matthew 7:7–8).

Unfortunately, what happens all too often is that we don't ask. As a result, we often deprive ourselves of many blessings (including miracles) that God is prepared to give us. Mary understood the value of intercessory prayer. As evidenced by her actions at the wedding in Cana, she knew exactly what to do when a major problem arose. She presented it directly to her Son and allowed him to handle it. After Jesus ascended into heaven, we see evidence that Mary continued that practice. Along with the Apostles, Mary devoted herself to prayer. Shortly after we hear of their spiritual practice, Luke writes that "they were all filled with the holy Spirit and began to speak in different tongues, as the Spirit enabled them to proclaim" (Acts 2:4). Obviously their prayer was very effective. Even though Jesus promised the Holy Spirit would descend on the Church (Acts 1:8), he never specified that it would happen without prayer. Mary and the Apostles knew what they were doing when they devoted themselves to prayer.

While this final biblical glimpse of the Blessed Mother illustrates her belief in the power of prayer, it also reveals much more. Note that she wasn't praying alone but joined the disciples in praying "with one accord." They were all gathered together in the upper room, united in prayer. Keeping in mind that the Apostles were the leaders of the Church, it's apparent that Mary had a special place in her heart for the institution founded by her Son. On November 21, 1964, Pope Paul VI closed the third session of the Second Vatican Council by proclaiming Mary "The Mother of the Church." As members of the Church, we should be comforted by the fact that the Blessed Mother is praying for each one of us. As we struggle to do the right thing and follow the Lord's commands, Mary is always ready to help us. Just as she looked out for the bride and groom at Cana and prayed with the disciples, she can help us to obtain the graces we need.

As we look at biblical stories of individuals being healed by Jesus, we're reminded that we shouldn't hesitate to ask for what we need. The Lord encouraged us to ask and gave us a great example as he petitioned the Father for various needs (John 17:11, Luke 23:34, Matthew 26:39). What we should be careful about, however, is only requesting material goods. While Jesus certainly knows we need things (food, money, good health), he urges us to place more emphasis on spiritual treasures (Matthew 6:32–33). How often do we seek the graces needed to lead a holy life? How often do we pray for an increased faith or the ability to control our temper? How often do we pray for an increase in the gifts of the Holy Spirit? Probably not as much as we should. In a world that constantly reminds us that "more possessions = more happiness," it's easy to lose sight of our spiritual needs. We sometimes forget that our true home is heaven, and we're only on this planet for a relatively short time. If we turn to our Blessed Mother and ask for the graces necessary to lead a good life and for the ability to resist temptation, she won't let us down. Just as she did throughout her life and culminating with her prayerful sessions in the upper room, she'll obtain for us the graces we need. All we have to do is ask.

Holy Mary, Mother of God, pray for us sinners now, and at the hour of death. Amen.

The Message: Prayer is always effective. Mary prayed, St. Paul prayed, and Jesus is often seen praying in the Gospel narratives. While we may not receive what we want, we'll always receive what we need. Although there's nothing wrong with praying for material goods, we should never forget to pray for spiritual graces.

Reflection Questions

1. Do you believe God can still perform miracles? Do your prayers reflect that belief or do you sell God short?

2. Why do you think our last glimpse of Mary in the New Testament has her in prayer? What can you deduce from the fact that she wasn't praying by herself but with the disciples?

3. Think of some spiritual graces you need and commit to pray for them daily. Remember to pray for the graces you need but which are unknown to you.

4. Have you asked our Blessed Mother to intercede for you in the past? If so, what were some results?

5. After Mary and the disciples prayed, the Holy Spirit descended on the Church. Read the biblical account of the first Pentecost (Acts 2:1–13). Then picture the scene and imagine you are there. What is the effect of the Holy Spirit's presence in your life? Do you sometimes resist the Spirit's power?

Conclusion

We've looked at Mary's words in Scripture. We've studied some of her appearances. And even though she undoubtedly said and did many other things over the course of her life, these are the ones God wanted recorded. In this book, I've tried to give you some reasons why Mary's words and actions are important. Could there be other lessons to learn by studying our Lady's appearances in the Bible? You better believe it! That's why I encourage you to continue reading over her words and focusing on those occasions where the inspired writers mention her name. By prayerfully doing so, you'll be able to uncover messages that are spoken directly to you. As with my other book, *A Worrier's Guide to the Bible*, I'd like this book to be a be a beginning rather than an end. The beautiful thing about Scripture is that, each time you read it, a different message can emerge. The Bible is the living, breathing Word of God, and by repeatedly examining Mary's words and actions, you will continue to get new and exciting insights.

We saw how she trusted, suffered, obeyed, and prayed. We read about how she was visited by the angel Gabriel who asked her to become the Mother of the Savior. We felt her confusion as she asked a question and marveled at her courage when she said "yes." In our minds, we contemplated how she broke the news to Joseph and her family. Due to an endless stream of illustrations and Christmas movies, we can picture the details of the night when Jesus was born in Bethlehem. But as we study the biblical details in greater depth, we start to realize that maybe that night wasn't as picture perfect as our manger may tell us. Mary must have been really uncomfortable, just like when she traveled to visit Elizabeth. Somehow she didn't let her lack of comfort stop her from doing the right thing. It's apparent that following God's will was the most important thing in her life. Even on the day when Simeon rejoiced at his encounter with the Savior, Mary experienced sorrow. She was told that suffering would be a big part of her life. That suffering becomes obvious to us when, twelve years later, Jesus reminds Mary and Joseph of his ultimate mission: to fulfill the Father's will.

Can you imagine how much those words must have stung? By the time Mary stood under the cross on Calvary, she had no doubt suffered many times. However, what amount of suffering could prepare a mother to witness what she saw that day? Her beloved Son was put to death by the very people he came to save. When we see Mary one final time, it's with her beloved Son's disciples, praying for the Church he founded.

Looking carefully at these events in the life of Mary tends to make us feel a little sorry for her, doesn't it? After all, it doesn't sound like she had a lot of fun. No matter how hard we look, we aren't going to find a lot of feel-good stories about Mary contained in the pages of the Bible. There aren't any recollections of cozy dinners with the Holy Family or tales of long walks with her husband. How about her joy at celebrating young Jesus' first birthday or how she loved the drawing he made for her? In spite of this apparent lack of fun events in our Lady's life, we do know she was joyful. In her words to Elizabeth, Mary rejoiced (in her Savior) and considered herself blessed. Somehow she was able to find joy and peace in the midst of her difficulties and suffering.

Can we assume Mary never had any pleasant things happen in her life? Of course not. But we can conclude that what we know about Mary is what God wanted us to know. Consider for a minute how amazing it is that a young woman can rejoice and feel blessed even though her life has been turned upside down. It could be there's a lesson for us here.

Mary had great faith and a desire to do God's will, no matter how difficult it was. As evidenced by her charitable journey to visit Elizabeth, she thought of others before she thought of herself. Just like many of us, her life involved some unpleasant chapters. She suffered, she was confused, and she was inconvenienced, but still she kept going. She knew God had a plan for her, and she continued to discern and follow that plan throughout her life. If you're like me, you probably struggle to do this every day. We wonder what the Lord wants us to do in a given situation. Sometimes it is even more painful when we know what he wants us to do, but we don't want to do it. By her example, Mary teaches us what it means to be faithful disciples. She reminds us it is possible to rejoice and consider ourselves blessed even when troubles arise. As we look at her praying with the disciples, we're reminded of the importance of prayer. Looking at her life makes us realize we have some work to do in our own lives, but we know there's hope. Just like us, Mary was human. Although highly favored by God and conceived without the stain of original sin, she was not divine. Mary was a creature, and that should inspire us. With God's help, we can all imitate her virtues.

I hope that reading this book will help you to admire Mary as much as I do. By meditating on the details in her life, it's pretty apparent she was one special woman. When you look at how she handled the various issues in her life, it's easy to look at her with admiration. As you reflect on the fact that her "yes" allowed the Word to become flesh, her importance grows. Thirty-three years later, that importance exploded off the charts as the Son born from her assent redeemed all of humankind. If you throw some Marian prayers into the mix, there's a really good chance that you're going to fall in love with her. If that doesn't seal the deal, wait until you start seeing the effects of her intercession in your life. You'll discover, as I have, that Mary cares deeply about each of us and desires to bring us closer to her Son.

Although I'd be happy if your admiration for Mary grew after reading this book, I'd be disappointed if that's the *only* thing that resulted from it. And I think I can say with total confidence that Mary and Jesus would also be a little disappointed. While we should admire Mary for the way she lived her life, there's one more thing we should strive to do: *Imitate her.* That, my friends, is the ultimate goal of this book. By looking at Mary's life we have a guidebook for what it means to be a Christian. Through her words and actions, the Blessed Mother serves as a human catechism who provides instructions for daily living.

Best of all, Mary is available 24/7 to help us as we attempt to follow in her footsteps. She has successfully dealt with the challenges of life and emerged victorious. How do we get in touch with her? The answer is simple. All we have to do is turn to her and ask her to help. She understands the importance of remaining close to Jesus and will do whatever she can to assist us. If you're not used to speaking to her, don't fret. Mary already knows who you are and has been keeping an eye on you, just as she did with the bride and groom at Cana. Make the decision to ask for her help today. If you're not sure what to say, start with the Hail Mary or some of the other prayers at the end of this book. If you'd rather make up your own words, that's fine, too.

As you grow closer to her and continue to meditate on her words and actions in the Bible, you'll see she will provide suggestions on becoming a better Christian. When she does, the best advice I can give you is, *Listen to Your Blessed Mother.*

Selected Marian Prayers

Through the centuries, there have been many prayers composed to honor the Blessed Mother. Here are a few of the most popular. By no means is this an exhaustive list, but it's a good start. If you're not used to conversing with Mary in prayer, these words will help you to get started. Whether you use these traditional prayers or your own words, the important thing is that you're speaking to your heavenly Mother. As time goes on, the words will flow more naturally and your relationship with her will grow.

Hail Mary

Hail Mary,
Full of Grace,
The Lord is with thee.
Blessed art thou among women,
and blessed is the fruit
of thy womb, Jesus.

Holy Mary,
Mother of God,
pray for us sinners now,
and at the hour of death.
Amen.

The *Memorare*

Remember, O most gracious Virgin Mary, that never was it known that anyone who fled to thy protection, implored thy help, or sought thine intercession was left unaided.

Inspired by this confidence, I fly unto thee, O Virgin of virgins, my mother; to thee do I come, before thee I stand, sinful and sorrowful. O Mother of the Word Incarnate, despise not my petitions, but in thy mercy hear and answer me.

Amen.

The Angelus

The Angel of the Lord declared to Mary:
And she conceived of the Holy Spirit.

Hail Mary, full of grace, the Lord is with thee; blessed art thou among women and blessed is the fruit of thy womb, Jesus. Holy Mary, Mother of God, pray for us sinners, now and at the hour of our death. Amen.

Behold the handmaid of the Lord:
Be it done unto me according to Thy word.

Hail Mary . . .

And the Word was made Flesh:
And dwelt among us.

Hail Mary . . .

Pray for us, O Holy Mother of God:
That we may be made worthy of the promises of Christ.

Let us pray:

Pour forth, we beseech Thee, O Lord, Thy grace into our hearts; that we, to whom the incarnation of Christ, Thy Son, was made known by the message of an angel, may by His Passion and Cross be brought to the glory of His Resurrection, through the same Christ Our Lord.

Amen.

The Magnificat

My soul proclaims the greatness of the Lord;
my spirit rejoices in God my savior.
For he has looked upon his handmaid's lowliness;
behold, from now on will all ages call me blessed.
The Mighty One has done great things for me,
and holy is his name.

His mercy is from age to age
to those who fear him.
He has shown might with his arm,
dispersed the arrogant of mind and heart.

He has thrown down the rulers from their thrones
but lifted up the lowly.
The hungry he has filled with good things;
the rich he has sent away empty.

He has helped Israel his servant,
remembering his mercy,
according to his promise to our fathers,
to Abraham and to his descendants forever.

Luke 1:46–55

Hail, Holy Queen

Hail, holy Queen, Mother of mercy, our life, our sweetness and our hope. To thee do we cry, poor banished children of Eve. To thee do we send up our sighs, mourning and weeping in this valley of tears. Turn, then, most gracious advocate, thine eyes of mercy toward us, and after this, our exile, show unto us the blessed fruit of thy womb, Jesus. O clement, O loving, O sweet Virgin Mary.

V. Pray for us, O holy Mother of God.
R. That we may be made worthy of the promises of Christ.

The following prayer may be added after the Hail, Holy Queen:

Let us pray. Almighty and everlasting God, Who by the working of the Holy Spirit didst prepare both body and soul of the glorious Virgin Mother, Mary, that she might deserve to be made a worthy dwelling for Thy Son, grant that we who rejoice in her memory, may, by her loving intercession, be delivered from present evils and from lasting death, through the same Christ our Lord. Amen.

Regina Coeli

Queen of Heaven, rejoice, alleluia.
For He whom you did merit to bear, alleluia.

Has risen, as he said, alleluia.
Pray for us to God, alleluia.

Rejoice and be glad, O Virgin Mary, alleluia.
For the Lord has truly risen, alleluia.

Let us pray. O God, who gave joy to the world through the resurrection of Thy Son, our Lord Jesus Christ, grant we beseech Thee, that through the intercession of the Virgin Mary, His Mother, we may obtain the joys of everlasting life. Through the same Christ our Lord. Amen.

About the Author

Gary E. Zimak founded Following the Truth, a lay apostolate dedicated to teaching the truths of the Catholic faith. He is a popular speaker at parishes and conferences, hosts a daily radio show on BlogTalkRadio, and is a regular guest on the *Son Rise Morning Show* and *Catholic Connection* with Teresa Tomeo, both on EWTN. Gary also authored *A Worrier's Guide to the Bible: 50 Verses to Ease Anxieties.*